THE OPTIMISTIC QUADRIPLEGIC

Ten Years and Counting

MY STORY OF FAITH, HOPE AND LOVE

by

KEITH STONE

The Optimistic Quadriplegic

Second Edition

Copyright 2025 by Keith Stone

ISBN 979-8-9985305-0-0

Dedication

To Sarah, I love you more today than yesterday but less than tomorrow!

Although the circumstances may be sad, my story is not. Mine is a story of optimism and all the people I met along the way including God. This is also love story. My wife, Sarah, and I had been married for 28 at the time of my accident. In the years since my accident, she has never left my side, sometimes literally. She is my sole caregiver. She is my rock. I can be a difficult patient with many demands but she has never wavered and she's always been there for me.

Table of Contents

CHAPTER 1

The Accident

"I can't move my arms or my legs. I can't move my arms or my legs." Those were my first words as a quadriplegic. It was August 16, 2015. My name is Keith Stone.

I had just finished my second round of golf for the day and my cart partner, Greg Gielarowski (Gil) and I were headed back to the car to meet up with the rest of our group. It was the biggest golf weekend of the year with 15 of my closest friends. I was driving and must have taken a wrong turn somewhere. We had to cross a large concrete and grass area to get back to the cart path that would take us to the parking lot. Parts of this cart path had four-inch-high curbs on the sides of them. Nothing that I felt was consequential. I was anxious to get to dinner and was probably driving faster than I should have. Gil didn't like my rate of speed and yelled out, "We're coming in hot!" I must have hit one of the curbs.

My next recollection is one that would change my world forever. I was lying face down on a grassy area with my left arm just inches from my face. When I tried to get to my feet, I realized that I could not move or feel my arms or my legs. I can't fully describe how eerie it was to see my own body part lying right in front of my face unable to make it respond to my brain's commands. It was the strangest feeling I have ever had in my life. Everything was happening so quickly there was very little time to dwell on that. Somehow, I had the clarity of mind to yell out, "I can't move my arms or my legs. I can't move my arms or my legs!"

Since there were no witnesses to the actual accident, I am left to speculate as to what exactly happened. I do know that the cart tipped over on the driver's side. All I can conclude is that I was ejected out of the cart just enough to have the roof of the cart come down onto the right side my neck.

We call the group I was golfing with the Griswolds. That name comes from the National Lampoon Vacation movie's main character Clark W. Griswold. We were all like-minded men in our mid-50s. We enjoy golf, beer and mercilessly ripping on any perceived weakness in a fellow Griswold. We all have children in the same age range and are just now starting to become empty nesters.

The Griswolds are a fairly organized group. We have our own logo; a moose based on Marty Moose, also from the Vacation movies. We have a slogan, "I'm in!" This is the expected response when an e-mail is sent out informing the group that a tee-time has been scheduled for the upcoming weekend. We have flags that we attach to the golf carts for all tournaments. We also have a website which contains all of the past results from our different tournaments.

We had gathered for the weekend at Boyne Highlands golf resort in Harbor Springs, Michigan. This annual tournament consisted of four rounds of golf and was called the Classic. The 2015 event marked the 19th playing of the Classic.

The group before Gil and I had completed unloading their equipment into their car and were driving their golf cart to the cart return area. After the accident, Joe Roe was the first Griswold on the scene. By this time the golf cart had been lifted off of me and the Boyne Highlands employee on the scene, the cart boy, was calling 911. Coming upon the scene, it was apparent to Joe that I was hurt and needed immediate medical care. He called 911 from his cell phone as well. Bob Chapman (Chappy) and Pat Donnelly were next to arrive. They immediately noticed the lack of color in Joe's face. They saw Gil kneeling over me trying to talk to me in a frantic state. Chappy came running over to check on Gil and me. Chappy tried to control the chaos taking place. Gil was so distraught that he was unable to communicate with Chappy. At this point Chappy noticed a new person on the scene. This stranger immediately took charge of my medical care. Although Chappy didn't know who this person was, he could tell by his demeanor that he had some type of medical training. Later we discovered that he was a volunteer first responder who must have been in the area as he arrived so quickly. He took charge of the situation and when the ambulance arrived, he directed the EMTs as to how they should properly load me onto the backboard. He even had them rehearse this several times under his direction as they only had one chance to get it right. To this day, neither Chappy nor I have been unable to identify who this person was, but will forever be grateful for his quick actions. I believe he was an angel sent to me by God to watch over me.

According to the Griswolds on the scene, the paramedics worked very quickly and I was in a neck collar, on a backboard with an IV running within minutes of the paramedic's arrival. I remember nothing about the ambulance ride. Steve Morman (Mo) and Pat Donnelly rode with the sheriff to the hospital. Chappy and Gil followed close behind by car.

My next recollection was talking to a man who told me that I was in the emergency room at McLaren Northern Michigan Hospital in Petoskey, Michigan. He introduced himself as Dr. Chaim Colen and he told me he was the surgeon on call. In a situation like this, obviously I couldn't pick my doctor. However, I was blessed that this small hospital in remote northern Michigan had a world-class neurosurgeon on staff. Dr. Colen was a 43-year-old graduate of the University of Puerto Rico School of Medicine. This included a rotation at Harvard Medical School. He did his post-graduate internships at Wayne State University in Detroit, Michigan. He had been on staff at McLaren Northern Michigan Hospital since 2009. At this time, I had no idea what a lasting impact he would have on my life and the lives of my family.

After going through a variety of tests including an MRI, Dr. Colen came in to talk with me about the results and the plan of action he would need to take. I don't have a great recollection of what Dr. Colen looked like this night, all I could remember was the different type of hat he had on. I refer to it as an English racing hat. I don't know why that stuck with me. It is one of those weird little things that got my attention. Dr. Colen did not pull any punches as he explained my condition to me. He told me I had fractured two of my vertebrae located at the C-4 & C-5 level. In addition, I had a 360-degree compression of my spinal cord at C-3. Vertebrae are grouped into sections. The higher that the injury was to the spinal cord, the more paralysis would occur.

C-4 & C-5 are very high on the spinal cord. Injuries this high generally result in quadriplegia. This means paralysis in the arms, hands, trunk and legs. The C-3 level of the spinal cord control respiration. Having the compression at C-3 but being able to tell everyone not to move me probably saved my life. MIRACLE # TWO!

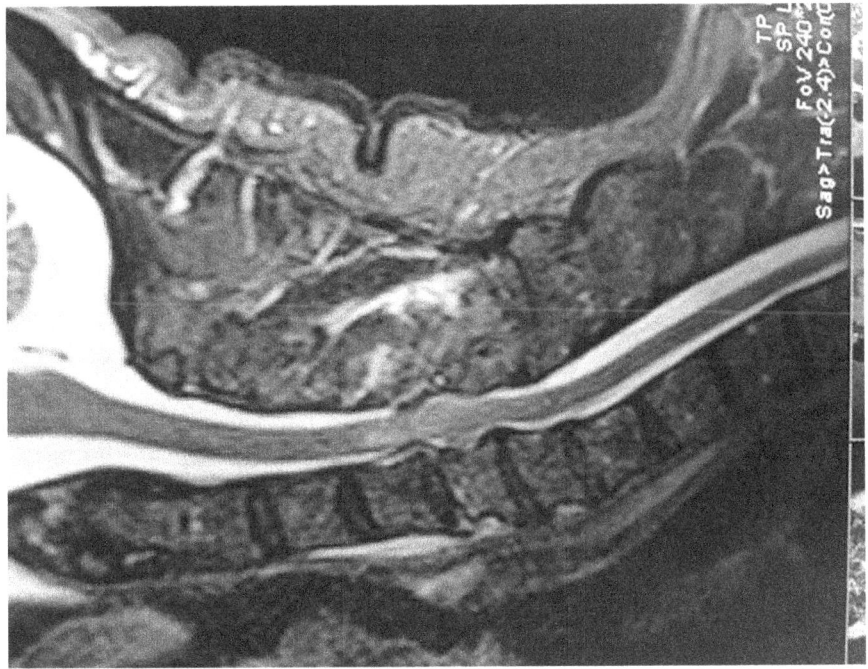

Initial X-Ray

Dr. Colen made it clear to me that there was a possibility that I would not survive surgery. My biggest concern that I had and I expressed this to him, was that I did not want to live the rest of my life dependent upon a ventilator to breathe. He took this very seriously and he promised me that he would do everything possible to avoid this. Even through all of this devastating news, I felt an overwhelming sense of peacefulness and calm. How could this be possible when facing news of this type? I credit the presence of God as I am sure He was there with me as I laid in the emergency room receiving all of this information. As we wrapped up our conversation, I asked Dr. Colen to be Superman. He made no promise that he could do that. He said he would try his best to have a successful surgery. I wasn't satisfied with that and I begged him to "please be my Superman".

A calming influence that night was the emergency room nurse, Peg. She had a very melodic voice and a warm personality. This made me feel relaxed in her presence. Her stated goal was just to do whatever I needed to make me comfortable. Whether that was a blanket or a conversation, whatever I needed. We had such quick interactions, but they meant so much to me during this very dark time.

The hospital also had a pastor on call, Pastor Ed Warner. Pastor Warner was a kind, soft spoken man that prayed with me while I was awaiting surgery. This helped bring a sense of peace and acceptance. I knew that I was okay with God and that I had turned everything over to Him. Pastor Warner continued to visit and pray with me throughout my stay at the hospital.

I drifted in and out of consciousness while Chappy, Gil, Mo and I waited for medical personnel to take me to surgery. Donnelly chose to stay in the waiting room. My number one concern as I laid there, was for the welfare of Sarah. I told each of them that no matter what happened to me they had to make sure that Sarah was well taken care of. I also told them my wishes of not wanting to rely on a ventilator to live. Just like any normal person, at no time in my life had I ever considered this. However, now that I was faced with the possibility, I was perseverating on the fact that I could possibly need a ventilator for the rest of my life.

I also told my three friends that if I died, I did not want to have a Stonerfest golf tournament in my memory. This relates back to one of the Griswolds tournaments, which is held in memory of Jeff Stemberger. He was one of the original Griswolds and I had known him since third grade. Jeff had esophageal cancer and suffered through that for several years. He died in 2006 at the age of 43. From that year on, we celebrated his life by playing a golf tournament called Bergerfest. We played this near the anniversary of his death in the first weekend of October. To further his memory, we imbibed in two of his favorite things; Towne Club pop and Pizza Rolls. I loved Jeff and I love the idea of the tournament to continue in his memory. So, I'm not sure why I was so against a Stonerfest. But, as I laid in the emergency room, I most certainly was.

Despite it being the darkest night of my life, there was still a moment of humor. Gil had a reputation among the Griswolds as the worst golf cart driver of the group. He had had a couple of incidents over the years, the biggest being him running into a tree which caused the roof of the golf cart to fold forward onto itself. I asked Gil to lean in and I told him "You're off the hook. I am now the worst golf cart driver".

Dr. Colen wanted to perform surgery as soon as possible. He also wanted to make sure that my loved ones were informed of my condition. Together, we called Sarah. That, obviously, was the most difficult conversation I have ever had. After Dr. Colen spoke to Sarah, explaining the severity of my condition, he then had me speak to her one last time before my surgery. I tried to keep my composure. No one ever plans to have a conversation like that. The call was short and painful, like ripping a Band-Aid off. I told her how sorry I was that this happened, that I loved her, and once again requested that I not be kept alive on a ventilator.

*"There are no atheists
in foxholes"*

—Ernie Pyle, ***battlefield journalist***

CHAPTER 2
Sarah Gets The News

This is how Sarah remembers that night.

My new school year had started as hectic as every other year. On that Sunday I wasn't feeling well and had decided to go to bed early. Keith was away on his golf trip, so it was just me at home. I stood up to head to my bedroom when my cell phone rang. I didn't know the number displayed, but something told me I better answer the phone.

"Sarah, it's Bob Chapman." My mind began to race. Why would Bob Chapman be calling me?

Bob was calling to tell me that Keith had been in an accident. I could tell by the tone of his voice that what he had to tell me was serious. Bob explained that Keith had fallen out of the golf cart he was driving and was seriously hurt. He explained that Keith was in the emergency room being evaluated by the doctor. He told me that Keith was unable to feel his arms or his legs. The emergency staff had told Bob that Keith's injuries were critical.

After hearing from Bob that Keith was in the emergency room, I grabbed my keys and headed to the car as he continued talking to me. Bob said that Keith was going down for more tests. He said that he would call me when he had more information. I told him that I was on my way to Petoskey but it would take me at least four hours to get there. After reminding me to drive safely, Bob told me that he would take care of Keith until I arrived. Those were the most important words to me.

After hanging up the phone with Bob, I immediately called my sister Carmela. Carmela has over 30 years of experience as a cardiac and critical care nurse in a teaching hospital. She has always been my first phone call when looking for an answer to any medical question. With her background I was sure she could help me. Carmela gave me a couple of great questions to ask the doctor. She said it was important to know what the surgeon hoped to get from performing the surgery on Keith. She also recommended that I ask the surgeon what he would consider a successful surgery. After reassuring me and telling me she loved me, I told her I would call her when I had more information.

After speaking to Carmela, I then called Keith's parents. This is one of the most difficult phone calls I had ever had to make. I dialed Jack and Agnes' number and braced myself. I knew I had to stay as calm as possible, but be intentional in my voice to relay that this was a very serious issue. Jack answered the call. I took a deep breath and said, "Dad, I have some news to share with you about Keith". I went on to explain what I knew. I also told them that I was on my way to the hospital and would share more information after I arrived. Surprisingly, even after receiving my phone call that late that night, Jack was quick to understand the seriousness of the situation. I promised to call back as soon as I knew anything more. He said that he and Agnes would start heading to Michigan first thing in the morning. He insisted that he still wanted me to call him back with an update no matter what time it was.

One difficult call down. Now it was time to call our eldest son, Andrew. Andrew answered his phone and was happy to hear from me.

Andy was used to being up later and didn't seem to be surprised to receive a call for me at this hour. I tried very hard to stay strong and tell him what was going on. I took a deep breath, but couldn't say anything. As much as I tried, I couldn't say a word. I began crying so hard that Andy became very concerned. He kept asking, "Mom, what's wrong? Are you okay? Is Dad okay?" I finally answered weakly, "No, Dad isn't okay." The line was silent for a minute as I tried to pull myself together. I told him I was driving to the hospital in Petoskey. Andy lived in Novi, a suburb of Detroit. He offered to drive me but I told him I couldn't wait for him to get to me. I needed to get to the hospital and his father as soon as possible. Andy asked what he should do. I told him to call his brother, Matthew, who was living in Seattle. I told him to convince Matthew to get home as soon as possible. I didn't want to have to worry about Andy driving up to the hospital upset and tired, so I asked him to wait until the next morning. He agreed and told me that he and his girlfriend, Alyson, would leave first thing in the morning. It turned out that Andy had no such intention of waiting until the morning and immediately headed to the hospital with Alyson.

Shortly after starting my drive to Petoskey, my other sister, Gloria, called. Carmela had called Gloria at my request. Gloria has over two decades of experience working as a pediatric nurse and is also a nurse educator. Concerned about me making the entire drive by myself, she offered to meet me in Cadillac. Cadillac is approximately one hour from Petoskey. At this point, I just wanted to get to Keith, but I knew I couldn't get through this alone. I agreed to meet Gloria.

While making the drive, I tried to think of any friends that might be close to Petoskey. Anyone who could run over and be at the hospital for me until I got there. I immediately thought of our good friends, the Cronkrights. I texted them to see how far they were from Petoskey, since they have a place in northern Michigan. To my disappointment, they were not close to Petoskey at all. They offered to make the two-hour drive to Petoskey, but I declined. I asked them to pray for Keith and I promised to call them when I knew more. I then texted my good friend Tia, who also has a place up north. Her place was not close to the hospital either. She also offered to drive to Petoskey to be with me, but I told her I was fine. Again, I told her I'd be in touch when I knew more.

Gloria's husband, Rich, had driven her to meet me. Gloria got into the driver's side of my car and we took off for the rest of the trip. While she drove, I was in contact with Bob. He was at the hospital with three of Keith's friends. They were going to stay at the hospital until I got there. I was so happy that Keith was not alone.

As we progressed towards Petoskey, my cell phone rang. Again, it was a number I did not recognize but I prayed it was the emergency room doctor telling me that Keith's injuries weren't nearly as serious as he had first thought. I quickly realized that it was just the opposite.

"Hi Sarah, this is Dr. Colen. Keith's injuries are very serious. I am going to have to take him into surgery right away. He has fractured his vertebrae at C-4 and C-5. He also has a 360- degree compression on C-3. I need you to understand the severity of his injuries. It is very unlikely that your husband will ever walk again. It is also very likely that he will require a ventilator to breathe for him. He has made it very clear that he does not want to live if he requires a ventilator to breathe. This is very serious. Keith has already given me permission for the surgery. Do I also have your permission?"

"Yes, you do. Please keep Keith alive for me," I squeaked out.

"I'll do my very best," Dr. Colen said with a very soft voice.

"What should I tell our boys and his parents? They all live several hours away."

"I would tell them that they need to get here as soon as they can," replied Dr. Colen.

After speaking with Dr. Colen, which included him giving me his personal cell phone number and telling me to call him if I had any problems getting to the hospital, he handed the phone to Keith.

"Hi honey, I'm so sorry. I'm so sorry. I don't want to live on a vent. Don't let me live on a vent. Okay? I love you. Promise me you won't let me live on a ventilator." These are the last words Keith said to me before going into surgery. I told him I loved him and I did my best to promise him that I wouldn't let him live on a ventilator. In the back of my mind, I wondered if this was a promise that I would truly be able to keep. When you are faced with never seeing your husband alive, you will promise anything to give them hope. At a much younger age I, along with my siblings, had to honor a similar request for both my mother and father. Could I do it again?

I called Keith's parents and Andy again and updated them with the news that Keith was going into surgery soon. I also let them know that the doctor said Keith's injuries were very serious and it was possible that Keith would not survive surgery. They asked me to keep them informed and to call them when I knew anything more.

My phone rang with another unknown number. By now I was answering my phone no matter what. This time it was one of the hospital employees named Peg. Peg talked to me in such a calm voice. She told me that Keith went into surgery right at midnight. She shared that she would keep checking in on Keith and would be there to greet me when I arrived at the hospital. She told me that the surgeon working on Keith was the best surgeon they had. She also told me that if anyone in her family needed this type of surgery, Dr. Colen would be the one she would request for them. This made me feel so much better. Peg said she would do whatever I needed. She provided me with a number to call her if I had any questions before arriving to the hospital. Peg's calm voice and reassurance helped me take a deep breath. I continued my begging and bargaining with God. Would he listen? Would he answer my prayers?

Just before arriving to the hospital, I texted Bob to let him know we were close. When we parked the car, I saw Bob, Gil, Mo and Pat across the parking lot. Their faces told me a lot. Each man was visibly shaken up. Bob began telling me what he knew as we walked to the surgery waiting room. After answering my questions and seeing that Gloria and I were set up in the waiting room, they each gave me one final hug before taking off to be with the rest of the Griswolds back at the hotel.

Peg came into the surgery waiting room and introduced herself to my sister and I. She told us again that we have the best surgeon working on Keith. She told us it would be a long surgery and asked what we needed. At this point, I'm not sure what I needed other than to see my husband. Knowing that we might get cold in the waiting room, Peg brought us nice warm blankets and told us to let her know if we needed anything more. I was so very thankful that she had been there for Keith when he needed her.

Andy and Alyson arrived close to 3:00 A.M. They sat with Gloria and I. We all tried to keep a conversation going, but with our great concern for Keith, there was very little that could be said. We just didn't know what was happening or what the future held for us. After spending several hours in the surgery waiting room, I felt the need to get up and go somewhere. I couldn't stay in that waiting room doing nothing any longer. I found a hospital employee and asked them to direct me to the chapel. God and I were going to have a conversation right now.

I opened the door to the small chapel and walked inside. There was a small altar with a visitor's book, an opened bible and a few pews. I sat down in the front pew, looked around to make sure I was alone, and then I let God have it. I yelled, I cried, I begged, and I bargained. How could

Keith's time on Earth be done? Keith's job wasn't done. He needed to stay with us. We have so much we wanted to do. My boys needed their father. Our future grandchildren needed to know Keith. I needed Keith. When I had no more energy to cry, I stood up, wiped my face and told God it was in His hands. I would accept whatever He had planned for Keith. For the first time since getting the call from Bob, my heart didn't hurt and I felt I could finally take a breath.

I returned to the surgery waiting room and continued to wait for any update on Keith's surgery. I realized I had no idea what Dr. Colen looked like. I wanted to make sure I would recognize him the minute he entered the waiting room. I proceeded to do a Google search on Dr. Chaim Colen and was very impressed with all of his training. I took a very good look at his face and memorized what he looked like. I now had a face to put with the voice.

At approximately 6:30 A.M., a small statured man came into the waiting room and looked around. He had scrubs on and he appeared to be looking for someone. I realized this was Dr. Colen. I walked up to him with Gloria, Andy and Alyson following me. He then asked "The Stone Family?" We quickly nodded. I was surprised how relaxed I became when I saw Dr. Colen's smile. He guided us into a small conference room and began providing us with Keith's medical update. My mind kept telling me that Keith was okay but the words the surgeon kept saying didn't match. Dr. Colen told us that Keith had survived surgery and that was the first positive move since Keith had entered the emergency room. Dr. Colen went on to say that Keith was in very serious condition. He had survived surgery, but there was no guarantee that he would ever be able to live off of the vent. He then reminded all of us the promise he had made to Keith that he wouldn't prolong his life if he required a ventilator to breathe. He told us that we needed to understand that it was very likely that Keith would never walk again. He may never be able to move his arm or legs. He was a quadriplegic and wanted to make sure we understood what this meant. This was the first time I had ever heard the word said out loud, "quadriplegic". He went on to tell us how serious Keith's injuries were. He explained what it meant to have fractured C-4 & C-5 in his neck along with having a 360-degree compression on C-3. When Dr. Colen was done speaking to us, I looked at Andy, Alyson and Gloria and told them I did not want Keith to hear that he may never walk again. I would not put a ceiling on Keith's progress. Dr. Colen smiled at me and I asked him if I could give him a hug. I thanked him for doing all that he could to keep Keith alive and I was so thankful for his surgical skills and kind personality. I know he helped keep Keith calm and I truly believed that he, along with God, had kept the love of my life alive.

A few hours after speaking with Dr. Colen, we were allowed to see Keith in ICU. The nurses appeared very confident in their ability to take care of Keith. They were very accepting of our family and understood that we were trusting them with our greatest treasure. We were quick to let the nurses know that both of my sisters have a medical background so they could use medical terms when necessary and that my sisters would answer any questions I might have. The nurses were wonderful! They told us when we came in for our first visit that only two people could be in the ICU at a time. We were asked to stay for only 10 minutes every hour. When we weren't in Keith's room, we were in the ICU waiting room. Every hour, one of us would go to the phone and call the ICU desk to gain permission to go in and see Keith. After the first few hours, the nurses allowed more than two people in Keith's room. I was allowed to stay in the room at all times as long as I didn't disturb Keith. This allowed me time to hold his hand, speak to him and to pray to God for complete understanding of what was in store for us. I also asked God to completely heal Keith's injuries and to provide me with the strength I would need to help Keith. The rest of the family came in and out of Keith's room throughout the first couple of days. The first-time seeing Keith was emotional for everyone. It broke my heart to have Andy and Alyson see Keith in such a critical state. I wanted to be strong for them, but I was having a lot of trouble being strong enough for myself.

Andy took one of the biggest items off my plate. He kept in constant contact with his younger brother Matthew. Matthew was in Seattle working as an intern at Microsoft and was unable to leave right away. After speaking with Dr. Colen, I told Andy to tell Matthew he needed to get here ASAP. To my dismay, ASAP meant four days to Matthew!

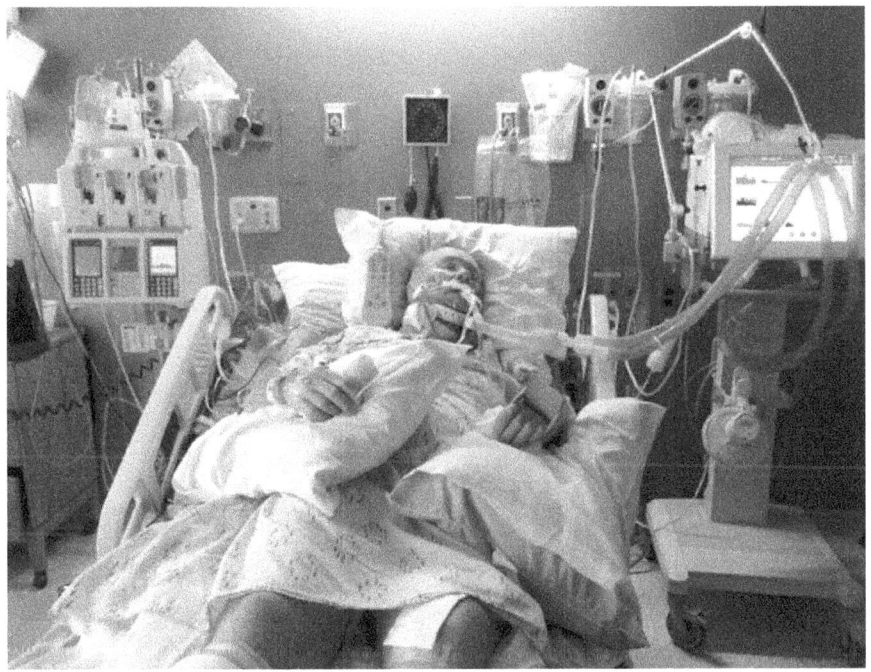

My first day in ICU

*People hear on the level you speak
to them from.
Speak from your heart,
and they will hear with theirs.*

—Marianne Williamson

CHAPTER 3
ICU

I was in surgery until 6:30 Monday morning. I didn't wake up until late Monday afternoon. When I woke up, the first person I saw was Sarah. I was so happy to see her. But, at the same time I felt so guilty for what I had put her through. As I slowly regained full consciousness, I became more aware of my surroundings. The first thing I noticed was the tube down my throat. It was irritating and I tried to pull it out. Carmela was there to intervene and with her assurances I was able to put up with it. What choice did I have? The tube upset me in a couple of different ways. The first was physically. Although this tube was breathing for me and providing life, I felt that it was inhibiting me from breathing. The tube also bothered me emotionally because I had asked Dr. Colen not to allow me to live on a ventilator. Of course, at that time, I didn't have all of the facts as to how long I might need this ventilator. But, in my mind, I thought I had issued a zero tolerance for a ventilator. Thankfully, the medical staff knew better than I did.

The next thing I noticed was how immobile my neck was. I was wearing a plastic collar that was keeping me from moving my neck too suddenly since it was in such a fragile state. I had a myriad of tubes coming in and out of my body. It didn't appear that anything above my neck was affected. I still had good vision, my thoughts were clear, and I could hear everything going on in the room. I had a tube going in my nose for nutrition as well as an IV for hydration. I didn't know it at the time, but I also had a catheter inserted, enabling me to urinate.

My experiences with intensive care units had been limited to what I had seen on TV. This was unlike anything I've seen on TV. The room seemed quite spacious. As I looked to the left there was the doorway to the hall which led to a nearby nurse's station. In front of me was a whiteboard which contained all of my information. There was also a sink, a mirror and the door to the bathroom. I could not see my reflection in the mirror so I did not know what I looked like. What made this room so dramatically different however, was when I looked to the right and saw the large picture window with a view of Bay Harbor which is part of Lake Michigan. I would imagine if this were a hotel, there would be quite a premium to pay for this calm and beautiful view.

I was under constant supervision by the nursing staff. It seemed like there was always a nurse in the room with me. At this point, all I really knew was that I had survived surgery and I was aware of my surroundings that included, most importantly, my beautiful wife. I didn't know what to expect, but it was a great joy for me just being alive! I still felt calm. At least I thought I was calm about my whole situation. I'm not really sure why I was so calm, until I remembered that God was with me and He would be guiding me through this whole ordeal.

I had always believed in God. As a kid we went to church regularly and after Sarah and I had the boys we were weekly churchgoers. Until this though, I don't remember having experienced God's presence. I don't remember where I heard it but there is an old adage that states "there are no atheists in foxholes".

I was informed later that it had been a restless night for the Griswolds back at the hotel. They slowly gathered for breakfast. Very little was said but they quickly decided that there was no way they could play the golf scheduled for that day. They all gathered their belongings and headed to the hospital to visit me. They had decided to take all the prize money for the weekend events and they gave it to Sarah. It was a much-needed and appreciated gesture, since Sarah had left home in such a hurry with very few clothes and very little money. Fifteen Griswolds stood in the waiting room, but not all of them were going to be allowed in to see me. Dave Brass and Steve Morman were the "lucky" two selected by the group and they got to see the upsetting situation I was in. Dave remembers the visit like this:

"I remember you were trying to acknowledge us. You had the tubes in that made it impossible. I was amazed at how brave and strong Sarah and Andy were. Mo and I were talking to you. I was on your left side he was on your right. Sarah was standing closer to your head. I remember 100% you squeezing my hand with your left hand. I took that as a great sign that you knew we were there and you were fighting strong. Of course, It was far too early to know everything at that point. They would not let us stay long, but we exchanged hugs and 'I love yous'. We told the guys in the waiting room what was going on. We all hugged Sarah goodbye and made sure that she knew that if there was anything she needed, anything, she would only need to ask once. We all filed out for the very somber drive home."

Dr. Colen, had flown to Florida soon after my surgery to take care of some family issues, so I would not see him until later in the week. However, he had called Monday from Florida to pass along my wishes to the staff to not be ventilator dependent. Sarah and Carmela had talked to me about the necessity for the vent. They got me to agree to stay on the ventilator for 7-10 days. The potentially tragic thing about my wishes for the ventilator was that I did not want to on one for the rest of my life like

Christopher Reeve. So, while Sarah convinced me stay on the vent for at least a week, I would have been okay to be on it for a much longer period of time as long as it wasn't permanent. My poor communication could have been very costly. Regardless, due to the wishes and instructions that Dr. Colen had passed on, the medical team had placed a high priority on doing everything in their power so that I wouldn't be ventilator dependent. Not needing a ventilator would take that troubling issue off the table.

On Tuesday afternoon they began that process. The medical staff put the vent on a standby mode which would only activate it if I was having any trouble breathing on my own. This process was repeated a few times throughout the day. The longest period in which I was able to breath with only limited help from the vent was four hours.

While being weaned off, I remember being scared just because of the unknown as to whether or not I would be able to breathe on my own. What would happen if I couldn't breathe on my own? This was the one thing I didn't want to have happen. But, the optimistic side of me was happy we were working towards my goal of breathing on my own because this is what I wanted to do. As they decreased the aid the machine was giving me, I was able to breathe on my own for longer periods of time. Hallelujah!! As time went by, however, I would get fatigued from breathing and Sarah and Gloria were there to remind me to breathe. At first, these cues came verbally. Later, Sarah was able to just touch my shoulder and that was enough to remind me to take a breath. As precarious as that may sound, there really was never a danger of me not breathing. I felt confident the whole time. My biggest problem was being able to take deep breaths rather than just shallow pants. Each time the ventilator was turned down, it became easier and easier for me to adapt.

With a ventilator tube in place, it was impossible for me to talk. However, I had a strong desire to be able to communicate with everyone. Carmela had come up with the idea of what we called the "Alphabet Game". The Alphabet Game was played like this: I would spell words by having a person read through the alphabet, when the letter I wanted was spoken, I would blink my eyes. One of the first questions I asked was, "Tell me everything the doctor said." Sarah, again, laid out how dire my prognosis was. In keeping with the decision Sarah had made earlier, she did not tell me that there was only a small percentage of chance that I would ever walk again.

It was great to be able to communicate, however it wasn't without some difficulties. Obviously, it took a great deal of time to spell out each word in a sentence. The first time the sound of laughter returned to our lives revolved around Sarah's inability to play the Alphabet Game patiently. If I was to indicate that the first letter of the word was a "W" rather than allowing me to continue to spell out the word, Sarah would yell out, "who, what, where, when, why". I'm sure this made sense to her but it was very frustrating to me. This was one of the first times that Sarah realized that I was "all there" because when she did this, I would give her what she calls the "idiot" look. Apparently, this is the look I shoot her when she says something that I think is dumb. I don't know what she's talking about, and I doubt that I ever do this. Although Sarah struggled with the Alphabet Game, Carmela, Gloria, Andy and Alyson picked up the slack and were excellent players.

The most important use of the alphabet game was when Sarah remembered that Matthew's tuition was due that week. I handled all the online transactions of this type so Sarah had no idea what needed to be done to make this payment.

Once of the most important life hacks you should take away from my story is this: *Always, always share your username and passwords for whatever accounts you might have with someone you trust!!*

Luckily, my cognitive abilities were still intact, and through the alphabet game, I was able to relay the information to Sarah so she could make the payment in time. What if I was still unconscious? What if I did not have the ability to communicate? This could have been a disaster. Don't make the same mistake we did.

While I was working hard to come off of the vent, many family members were working behind the scenes. Carmela and Gloria were able to answer all of our medical questions while also taking care of Sarah. Gloria's eldest son, Brandon, was setting up our CaringBridge blog. CaringBridge was an excellent way to communicate with our family and friends. They can log onto our site and be brought up to speed on my condition. This allowed us to tell the story only once but provided a way to let all of our friends and family know how I was progressing.

Another great use of the social media platforms was the ability to make massive requests for prayers. Prayer works! As I just told you, I had always considered myself a Christian but nothing close to devout. I know in my heart that God and the overwhelming number of friends and family that prayed for me made a huge difference in my recovery.

Between Facebook and CaringBridge, word of my condition spread fast. This began an overwhelming show of love. To this day, I can't believe the level of support we received from people and what a difference it made to Sarah and I. We received visits from friends and family members who were vacationing in the area. Sarah was the principal at Indian Hill Elementary school in Grand Blanc. Several of her teachers drove the 200+ miles to Petoskey just to see us. This really helped Sarah get through some very tough times. Sarah had based her life on making connections with people. Those connections were further demonstrated by a fellow Grand Blanc educator, Vickie. She reached out to Sarah to let her know that she had a vacation house nearby and that she wanted our family to stay there while I was in the hospital. Vickie had driven two hours out of her way to get the key to Sarah. This was just another example of how many people demonstrated their love and how willing they were to help. I have always believed that if you could boil the entire bible down to one message it would be "Love one another". I'm confident that the support and love we received from our entire community of friends made God very proud and proved to be a source of great strength for Sarah and me. We came across these lessons countless number of times during our journey and it is an example of the love that God has taught us. Dozens of Sarah's friends stopped by just to give her a hug. They didn't want to intrude with our important family time, but they understood how much a hug would mean to her.

Late Tuesday afternoon, my parents arrived from Florida. Sarah knew that seeing me on a vent would be a traumatic experience for them. She met them out in the waiting room. She explained what they were going to see and she offered to show them pictures so they could prepare to see their only child in such a vulnerable state. Defiantly, my dad refused, telling Sarah that they have seen plenty of people on a vent before. Sarah pleaded with them and told them that they had never seen their son on one before. However, they continued into my room to see me for the first time. I saw my dad walk in and instantly the color left his face and the strength left his legs. He started to collapse. This was heartbreaking for me. For my octogenarian parents, seeing me in this state must have been the most difficult thing they have had to do. Again, I felt guilty for putting them in this position. My Mom handled it much better. She was a rock for my dad.

Almost immediately, using the alphabet game I asked Sarah give my parents the message, "I'm going to be okay. Dad you need to be strong for me." This seemed to make them feel a little better and they were able to settle in and catch up on all of the events that had occurred to date.

After the weaning of the ventilator on Tuesday, we were told that the plan was to continue to lengthen the weaning period through Wednesday. When the on-call doctor came in Wednesday morning, he said that my respiratory numbers looked good and that he wanted to pull out the tube immediately. That was both exciting and frightening to me. Exciting because I wanted to get rid of the tube. Frightening because I feared I wasn't ready. I wasn't given any time to think about it as the tube was removed very quickly. I was able to breath on my own with normal oxygen assistance as needed.

However, there was one speed bump. The first thing I said to Sarah was "You SUCK at the alphabet game!" While it was great to have laughter in the room, it probably would have been better if I told her that I loved her first but many "I love yous" followed. This was a huge milestone in my physical and mental recovery. Now that I was able to talk, it was all non-stop catching up on my prognosis, determining how everyone else was handling my injury and just general appreciation for being alive. In hindsight, to be on the vent for only two days was incredible and that helped to speed up my recovery at a faster pace.

Early on, I told Sarah that what happened was devastating, but that I was going to make this into something positive. Right from the start, I developed an optimistic attitude and I wasn't going to look back at what could have been. This attitude has served me well throughout my journey. I am convinced that always looking forward and pushing towards the next goal, rather than looking back and wallowing in self-pity, was an important factor in my recovery. I believe God chose us for this journey. I certainly don't understand why, but I was determined to make the best of it and to be stronger because of this. People spend their whole life trying to find their purpose in God's plan, and I believe I had found mine.

Now that I was able to breathe on my own, the next step was to get me up as soon as possible and moving whatever parts of my body that I could. For the first time, since the accident, I was aware I was able to move my shoulders. This is normal for an injury at my level but that was about it. I was unable to move my arms or my legs. I only had minor sensation below my nipple line. One thing that kept me going was that when anyone squeezed my big toe, on either foot, I was able to feel that pressure. Whether it was a medical fact or not, we all took that to be a great sign.

On Thursday, my youngest son, Matthew, arrived at the hospital. He had been doing a summer internship at Microsoft. Luckily his internship was just about up and he was able to finish the last part of his project so he could return home a little early. Matthew has never been an outwardly emotional person so I didn't expect much when he saw me for the first time. As Matthew stood at the foot of my bed, Sarah asked him if he thought she had exaggerated the seriousness of my condition now that I was off the vent. Matthew agreed that he thought his mom had exaggerated just a little bit. It was great to have Matthew there. The whole family was together again, although under horrible circumstances.

One of the biggest challenges for any spinal cord injury patient is to be able to manage their blood pressure. In general, a spinal cord injury will lower the patient's blood pressure considerably. My blood pressure usually runs around 100/60, sometimes even lower. This is problematic when a patient tries to sit up but doesn't have the blood pressure to support consciousness. To that end, I was introduced to something called the "Cardiac Chair". This device started out flat like a bed. The nursing staff would transfer me over into the chair as it laid flat. Then, they would slowly raise my head and lower my feet until I could no longer tolerate my blood pressure deficiencies. We did this every day from Wednesday through the remainder of my stay. I tolerated it quite well the first day and I was able to sit in the chair for approximately two hours. As the days went on, I was able to keep upright for longer periods of time. I was grateful for any time out of my bed. The medical staff seemed pleased with my ability to handle the cardiac chair. It certainly was nice to be able to sit there and enjoy that beautiful view.

While in the hospital I was able to participate in some limited physical therapy. Sarah, Carmela and Gloria were shown how to stretch my hands and legs by one of the therapists and we did this many times throughout the day. They had started with this even before I regained consciousness because they were told how important it was for my recovery. On a couple of occasions three therapists came to my room and we would work on sitting on the edge of my bed. It was quite a team effort, considering my extreme lack of mobility and all of the tubes coming out of me, but I wouldn't give up nor would the therapists allow me. I was able to sit on the side of the bed for longer periods of time but I always required someone to support me.

By the end of the week, I was able to try solid food again. Or solid as far as the hospital was concerned. My first food was chocolate pudding. I then moved on to mashed potatoes and gravy, macaroni and cheese, and a chocolate shake. I was able to swallow these without any difficulty. I was put on a soft food only diet for the remainder of my stay.

On Friday, I had a visit scheduled with Gil. Gil, you'll recall, was riding in the cart with me when the accident happened. The last time I had talked to him was when I was in the emergency room. I know he was pretty upset at that time, and Bob had also told me that Gil was a mess the night of the accident. I didn't know how we were going to react to each other. My number one goal was to make sure that he knew that none of this was his fault and that he should carry no guilt whatsoever for what happened. The time arrived and Gil walked in and we both teared up. Everyone excused themselves from the room so Gil and I could have some time alone. Gil looked very concerned and I started with trying to assure him that there was nothing that he could have done. In fact, I even went on to thank him because Sarah had informed me that had he not been so adept at avoiding me when the golf cart tipped over, I could be in a lot worse shape. We talked for a couple of hours and I could tell as the conversation continued, Gil's heart lightened and he started to feel better about all of the events. He recorded a video message from me that he sent to all of the other Griswolds. As much as the meeting may have helped Gil, it helped me at least as much because I didn't want him to carry around any guilt. By the time he left that day, it appeared as if a thousand pounds had been lifted from his shoulders.

Gil was the first of many visitors I had. I'm not sure what people expected to see when they came to visit for the first time. I certainly wouldn't know what to expect. Each visitor seemed to feel better about my situation after talking with me. Everyone said how great I looked and they all seemed to leave feeling much better about my prognosis – exceeding the expectations they had before we had met. I was glad that I was able to provide people with that type of peace.

Over the weekend, Gloria's husband, Rich, who is normally a very low-key guy came into my room excited to tell me about an encounter he just had. Rich spent the majority of his time in the family waiting room since there was limited number of visitors allowed in my room at one time. Rich went on to say that he had taken up a conversation with another family. They were there visiting their mother who had suffered a heart attack. Rich shared the story as to why he was visiting the hospital. As he told my story one of those family members, a gentleman named Ron, look astonished. He told Rich, "I have to meet your brother-in-law. That was me 25 years ago."

Rich returned to my room and relayed the story. He asked if I wanted to meet with him. "Of course, I do. Is he in a wheelchair?"

Rich replied, "No, he's walking around just like I am".

I replied, "Then I have to meet him!"

Ron came into my room later that day and spoke to Sarah and I. He proceeded to share his story. While serving in the army in his twenties in Florida, he was involved in an accident in his pickup truck. He was ejected through the windshield with such force that he was propelled through a chain link fence. He woke up in a VA hospital, paralyzed with injuries to his spine very high, similar to mine. Sarah and I were shocked. How could this be? He's standing here right in front of us as if nothing had ever happened. Ron went on to explain that he spent several years in a VA hospital. He was on a ventilator for much longer than I was. He was also bed ridden for a much longer period of time than I would expect to be. He explained that currently, the only lasting impairment from the accident was that he would occasionally drop things out of his hands. He would tell himself big deal and just bend over and pick it up. Ron went on to explain that he has a career with the postal service. He walked a mail route for over twenty years. He went on to have a family and was now living in Western Michigan. This single meeting motivated me throughout my entire recovery process. Here's a guy who was injured at least as bad as I was, but was now walking around as if nothing had happened. This was the only time I met with Ron. We tried to set up meetings since then, but for various reasons we could not connect. I often times wonder whether Ron was real at all. By that, I mean, could he have been an angel sent to me to give me hope just when I needed it most? For him to be in that waiting room, to take up a conversation with my brother-in-law, to have the same injury as me, and yet to be fully recovered seems too coincidental to believe. I am convinced that that must have been another message from God. Years after the meeting I was told about a Bible verse that the friend who gave it to me, pastor Wentzel, thought might help me understand these interactions and found the following verse.

Do not forget to be kind to strangers and let them stay in your home.
Some people have had angels in their home without knowing.

—Hebrews 13:2.

CHAPTER 4
Leaving The Hospital

Since day one of my stay in ICU, Sarah and I knew that I wouldn't be able to spend the rest of my life at this hospital. The question we had was what would be the next step? The answer was a rehabilitation hospital. McLaren hospital had a social worker on staff whose duties included finding the right rehabilitation hospital for me. We hadn't had any discussions about this, but she was looking at rehab hospitals close to our home in Grand Blanc as anyone would expect. This included a hospital in Detroit, Rehabilitation Institute of Michigan and the University of Michigan hospital in Ann Arbor. I was pretty much out of all of these discussions but Sarah and her sisters were dealing with this. During one of the discussions, Sarah's sisters inquired about a rehab hospital that they were familiar with that was in Grand Rapids, which is closer to their homes in the Kalamazoo area. The name of this hospital was Mary Free Bed (MFB). Yeah, I thought it was a weird name the first time I heard it too. This hospital had a sterling reputation and when the social worker heard that we might be interested in going to MFB, she was very excited. She told Sarah, "That hospital would be perfect for Keith, but I didn't think you'd be interested since it is so far from your home."

Mary Free Bed was located in Grand Rapids, Michigan about two hours from Grand Blanc. Sarah told her that our first priority was to get me the highest level of care. The social worker told us that she would begin working on my admittance application right away. Sarah and I were puzzled by her use of the word "application".

We did some research and found that because MFB was such an excellent facility, beds there were in very high demand. It could be compared to a selective "magnet school" in which the school can choose its students. My records were submitted to MFB. By the following day we had heard back that MFB would have an opening on Tuesday. Both, the Petoskey Hospital and MFB agreed that I would be the perfect candidate. Now we knew where my future home would be. This was quite a load off of our minds. The more we researched the hospital, the more excited we got. Dr. Colen's partner, Dr. Harris, agreed that I should be ready for transfer on Tuesday. The timing was perfect, as Dr. Colen was scheduled to have returned by then and he would be able to sign my release papers.

I will forever be indebted to the nursing staff during my stay at Northern Michigan McLaren Hospital. In my short time spent with each of the nurses, I was able to latch on to a piece of their personality. I probably shouldn't have any favorites, but without a doubt, my favorite was nurse Tara. Tara worked a couple of night shifts with me and we shared a sarcastic sense of humor. We really enjoyed going back and forth with comments. Nurse Michelle was a soft-spoken sweetheart that explained everything to Sarah and I in as much detail as we requested. She even gave Sarah a head-start on learning things she would need to know as she became more involved in my care. I would also like to thank the other nurses, Vicki, Jamie, Lisa, Bobbi, Katie, Sharon, and Ashley. There are perhaps no greater critics of nursing care than Carmela and Gloria. They, being excellent nurses themselves, had very high standards. The best thing I can say about the nursing during my stay in Petoskey, was that Carmela and Gloria both thought the nursing staff was excellent. No higher praise could be given.

It was Tuesday morning, only nine days since my accident and it was moving day. Time for me to make the three- hour journey via ambulance to MFB. I heard a familiar voice and it made me smile. It was Peg, the nurse from the emergency room. She had come up to say goodbye. That was such a kind act for her to make. She gave Sarah and I several hugs and wished us well. The ambulance drivers were ready to go, but what we didn't have yet was a doctor to sign off on my release. I knew it would be Dr. Colen that was coming in and I was very excited to see him again as I hadn't seen him since the night of my surgery. He finally arrived and walked in and I couldn't help but smile as I greeted him by saying, "That's exactly how I remember you." By that I meant he had the same hat on that I remember from the emergency room. He smiled and leaned in to give me a hug. I had only talked to this man for 30 minutes of my entire life but I felt extremely close to him. He did after all, save my life, so I suppose that tends to make you close to another human being. He told me that he had been tracking my progress and was very pleased and even surprised by how well I was doing. We reminisced about our discussion regarding the ventilator. We were both glad that it was no longer an issue. I told him that someday soon I would WALK into his office to see him. He said he couldn't wait to see that happen. After some additional small talk Dr. Colen went about signing the paperwork to get me released. He reminded Sarah and I of his cell phone number and told us to contact him if we had any questions or concerns. Since then, we have texted Dr. Colen many times and he has always answered promptly. He even texted Sarah on Mother's Day. I am still awestruck by how such a gifted surgeon, who held my life in his hands, could be such a down to earth, friendly, regular guy.

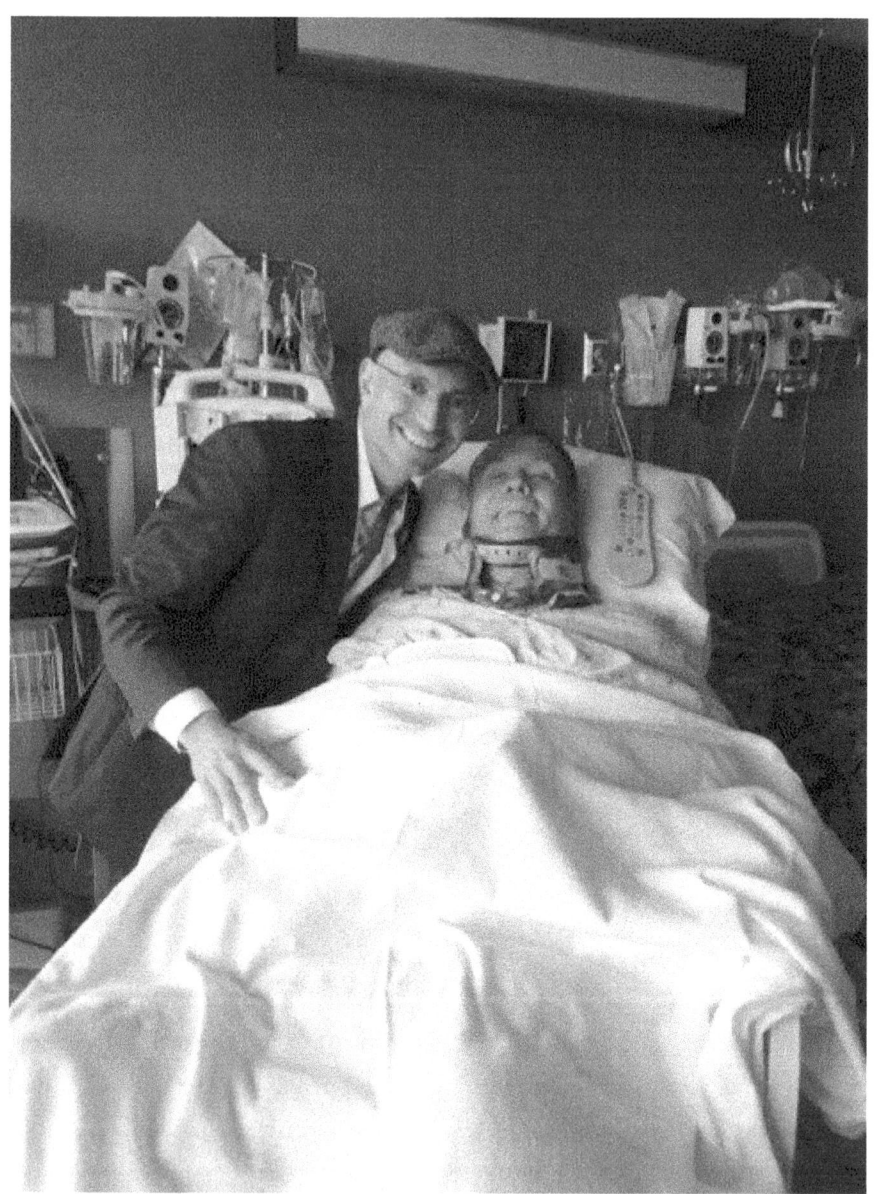

Dr. Colen: Neurosurgeon Extraordinaire

As I was transferred onto the ambulance gurney, I paused to consider my current condition. I have one plate and three bolts of metal holding my spine together. I was wearing a plastic neck collar twenty-four hours a day to immobilize my neck. Everything above my neck worked fine. I could see, hear, and speak normally. I only had movement in my shoulders. I could not feel any stimulus below my shoulders except in my big toe when it was squeezed. My blood pressure was still not 100% stable and if I were to sit up, I would have to have that monitored closely. My injury was incomplete which meant that the spinal cord was not severed. This gave me a great amount of hope because that meant there was a possibility that the nerves could regenerate and reconnect my body to my brain. All of these things helped provide me with a tremendous sense of optimism. However, what I didn't know was that I was given a zero to slim chance of ever walking again due to other tests that were run at the hospital. Sarah made the decision not to tell me that so it wouldn't limit the possibilities in my head. She made the right call. I'm glad she did that. As far as I was concerned, I was absolutely going to walk again and I had an extremely optimistic outlook. I was not afraid to share that with anyone. I said my goodbyes to Sarah and my parents. They were going to follow the ambulance to Mary Free Bed.

An optimist is a person who sees
a green light everywhere,
while a pessimist sees only
the red stoplight

—Albert Schweitzer

CHAPTER 5
Welcome to Mary Free Bed

As we headed down highway 131 to MFB, I felt a bit apprehensive for the first time. I determined that it was due to a fear of the unknown. I was excited to get started on my recovery but I really didn't know what that would entail. I expected my therapists to be similar to a group of drill sergeants at a Marine boot camp. I wasn't afraid of hard work. In fact, I welcomed it, but I just didn't know what this next step in the journey was going to look like.

Let's address the strange name of my future home, Mary Free Bed. I couldn't get past the fact of what an unusual name it was. Mary Free Bed was started by a women's guild in 1891. This group of women were concerned about healthcare for the poor in the Grand Rapids area. Taking advantage of the popularity of the name Mary at the time, anyone named Mary or if anyone knew a Mary, were asked to donate 10 cents to the fund. After a short while the group had gathered enough money to cover a free bed at a local hospital. Hence the Mary Free Bed name was born. Today, this group raises over $400,000 annually in support of the Mary Free Bed Rehabilitation Hospital.

When we arrived at the hospital on Wealthy Street, two attendants unloaded me and we headed into the hospital. We stopped at the front desk and we were informed that I had been assigned to room 3138. 3rd floor north held 24 beds was home to all of the spinal cord injury patients. As I was lying flat on my back on the gurney, I could only see the ceiling. When we exited the elevator on the third floor, I first noticed a beautiful glass light fixture. Orange and green colors shaped like flowers. It's funny how some things stick in your head. We rolled down the mostly empty hallway and arrived at my room. The ambulance attendants rolled the gurney next to a bed. Two nurses were immediately on the scene to help transfer me into my bed. Once that was complete, I bid the ambulance attendants adieu and they were back on their way to Petoskey.

The two nurses made sure I was comfortable and then went about explaining some of the features of the room. I was in a standard hospital bed. To my right was a sliding barn style door that led to a very large bathroom. The bathroom was completely flat and barrier free with a tile floor, a sink, a toilet. The bathroom floor was flush with the entrance to the shower so I could be easily rolled in. On the wall behind me was a bigger than life photograph of a forest scene. I couldn't ever see it, but I'm sure it made for peaceful scenery for my guests. At the foot of the bed, was a large flat screen TV. I watch a lot of TV, so I was very happy to see that. To the right of that was a board that contained a list of information. Including, who my doctor and nurses were, the day of the week and a space for my therapist's names. These had not yet been filled in. To the left of the TV was a large cabinet which had a lock on it for any personal items or clothing that I would need to store. On my left was a bright green couch that folded out into a bed. This would serve as Sarah's bed for the duration of our time here. (Remember earlier when I told you that she literally stayed by my side? I wasn't kidding) Sarah claimed it was comfortable but it didn't look like it to me. Above the couch was a long window from wall to wall. This window faced west and had a beautiful view of a church with magnificent spires. This church was St. Andrews which I found comforting since we had a son named Andrew. The church was lit up at night and always served as a source of peace for me. Just a few months prior to my arrival at MFB, an addition to the hospital was completed. This provided private rooms for patients rather than a double room that was the standard previously.

During those first few minutes there were several people coming in and out of my room. I'm sure I was introduced to them, but I don't recall very many of their names. One name that unfortunately did stick out was Paul who was in charge of much of the large medical equipment, more specifically wheelchairs. I was excited that they were already talking about getting me a wheelchair. However, while talking about me, without really talking to me Paul asked for confirmation that my injury was complete. The nurse confirmed that my injury was complete. This is the first time that I had heard that and I protested and became very upset. Paul never really addressed my concern, continued about his business and then left the room. At this time, Sarah and my parents arrived in my room. All this had happened in only about fifteen minutes. Sarah could tell that I was upset and wanted to know what was wrong. I told her that she had never told me that my injury was complete. Sarah responded by telling me my injuries were not complete. I went about telling her what had happened with Paul and the collective blood pressures in the room rose considerably. Sarah went about finding Paul and asking him what he thought he was doing. The situation was resolved and we received an apology from Paul. However, my first few minutes at my new home were less than ideal.

Throughout that first day I learned about the different people I would be dealing with during my stay. Dr. Ho would be overseeing my care. There were nurses who were assigned to approximately four rooms each. The nurses work 8 or 12-hour shifts. The staff that does most of the heavy lifting are the nurse techs. They do all of the literal dirty work such as toileting, showering, weighing, feeding, dressing or just about everything that a patient would need. We had a social worker assigned to our case as well.

Since I arrived at MFB, I had an irritating cough. It just felt like there was something caught in my lungs. After watching me fight this for several hours, one of the nurses finally announced, "We should go get Hillary." She was the first tech I had any interaction with. She came into my room and announced that she was going to perform something called a "quad cough." She did this by putting her fist on my sternum, similar to where you would put your first for a Heimlich maneuver. She told me to take a deep breath and as I did that she pushed down hard. Instantly, the irritant was loosened from its place and I was able to cough up the phlegm. I quickly asked her "Where have you been all day?" This was my first example of the many tasks that the techs will do for me during my stay.

After the excitement, I realized how tired I was. We expected pushback when we told the nurse that Sarah planned on sleeping on the couch next to me. On the contrary, two of the techs brought in everything she would need such as a blanket, pillow and sheet. We were told that this was commonplace at the hospital and everyone understood the importance of having a loved one nearby.

My first full day at MFB began with a visit from a tech to get me dressed. I quickly learned that there was no room for modesty for someone in my position. Since I couldn't dress myself, I was completely at the mercy of the techs. I had both male and female techs. That never bothered me. There were many times when I would be laying on the bed completely naked.

A new part of my daily ensemble would be items to help control my blood pressure. Spinal cord patients already have lower blood pressures than normal. A person with a fresh injury, such as mine, who had been lying flat on his back for such an extended period of time was especially vulnerable to low blood pressure issues. To combat that, I wore extremely tight stockings that were called TED hose. TED is short for "thromboembolism-deterrent". They were thigh high stockings that would help promote blood flow back up to my heart rather than allowing blood to pool in my legs and feet. Additionally, the TED hose were wrapped with ace bandages all the way from my toes to my thighs. Finally, I wore an abdominal binder. This was an extremely tight piece of fabric connected with Velcro placed around my torso. Like the TED hose, this was used to promote blood flow returning to my heart.

After getting dressed, my breakfast was delivered. I continued to have a soft diet. This meant scrambled eggs for me. For future meals I was able to order from a large selection. The orders were to be submitted a day ahead of time. This quickly became a stressful part of my day as the dietary staff was on us continuously to submit the forms. Sarah and I found it pretty comical but I'm sure they were sick of us for always being late with our selections.

It was now day two of my stay at MFB. Today, I would be evaluated by the various therapists. First to arrive was the speech pathologist. A speech pathologist does more than just make sure you can talk. They are also charged with making sure I can swallow properly and determined what type of diet I would be on. The speech pathologist also conducted cognitive testing. Examples of the cognitive tests included the following:

I would be told a story and then she would come back and ask me what occurred first, second or last in the story. There were also several math questions that I had to calculate in my head. There were many short-term memory tests in which I would be given a list and then asked to recite that list back. I blew away the speech pathologist with how well I did on the tests. She concluded that I wouldn't have to continue with speech nor did she have any concerns about my cognitive ability. This was welcome news to me as I wanted to devote my time to repairing my physical body and not using valuable time working on my mental abilities. As I was completing the required tasks, I could hear Sarah and my dad try to answer the questions along with me. They struggled to keep up and giggled to each other that they were glad that they weren't the one having to take these tests.

Next to arrive was a chipper blonde woman from occupational therapy (OT). Her name was Ashley. I would work with Ashley during my entire stay at MFB. We built quite a friendship. An occupational therapist is charged with getting patients full use of their arms and hands so that they could perform day-to-day tasks such as hygiene, dressing and feeding myself. She gave me braces for my hands to wear at night. They provided support and kept my fingers from curling into my palm. Ashley and I did a lot of work bending my hands and fingers to help them become more flexible.

After being seen by the OT, my lunch arrived. I felt quite helpless as my Dad would have to feed me on one side while my Mom provided a drink for me on the other. I sure was thankful to have them there. Although my parents were happy to help me out, I couldn't wait for the day when I could feed myself again.

After lunch, the physical therapist (PT) arrived. The PT's are mostly concerned with ambulation and large motor skills involving the legs. During their evaluation, they had me doing a lot of stretching to determine my baseline abilities. After stretching the therapist brought in a motorized wheelchair. I couldn't believe that they were already talking about putting me into a wheelchair. I didn't think it could happen that quickly. I became anxious not knowing how I was going to get out of my bed and into the wheelchair given my physical limitations.

The answer was on the ceiling above me. Hidden out of sight in the top cabinet at the foot of my bed was a motorized lift. This lift moves around the room on a track that was installed on the ceiling. A nylon sling was placed under me by rolling me from side-to-side on the bed. Four straps on the sling were then attached to the handles of the lift. The straps are my leg were crisscrossed to prevent me from sliding out of the sling. Then, with the use of a remote control, they were able to lift me up out of the bed. It was a very comfortable feeling that first time. I felt very safe even though I was eight feet off the ground. The sling was moved across the room to hover over the wheelchair. I was lowered down into the chair and then the sling was removed from underneath me through various manipulations. The sling was very smooth and it was easy to pull out. That lift and sling would be a very important part of my life during my stay at MFB.

While it was a great feeling to be sitting in the wheelchair, I quickly became aware that I wouldn't be able to drive it. I didn't have the motor abilities to control it just yet. I was only in the wheelchair for a short time when I felt my blood pressure drop. One of the techniques to fight this was to tip the wheelchair backwards so I was more parallel with the ground. This is also the technique that I would use to ward off pressure sores. Pressure sores are a source of great angst to anyone in a position in which they are unable to move. Without relieving the constant weight on just one part of your body, sores can develop that can take weeks and weeks to heal. I was constantly warned about pressure sores by all of the hospital personnel and how to combat them. In the future as I spent more time in the wheelchair, I was told to stop everything I was doing every fifteen minutes to tip back so as to combat potential pressure sores. I was given a stop watch that was set to ring every fifteen minutes to help me with this process.

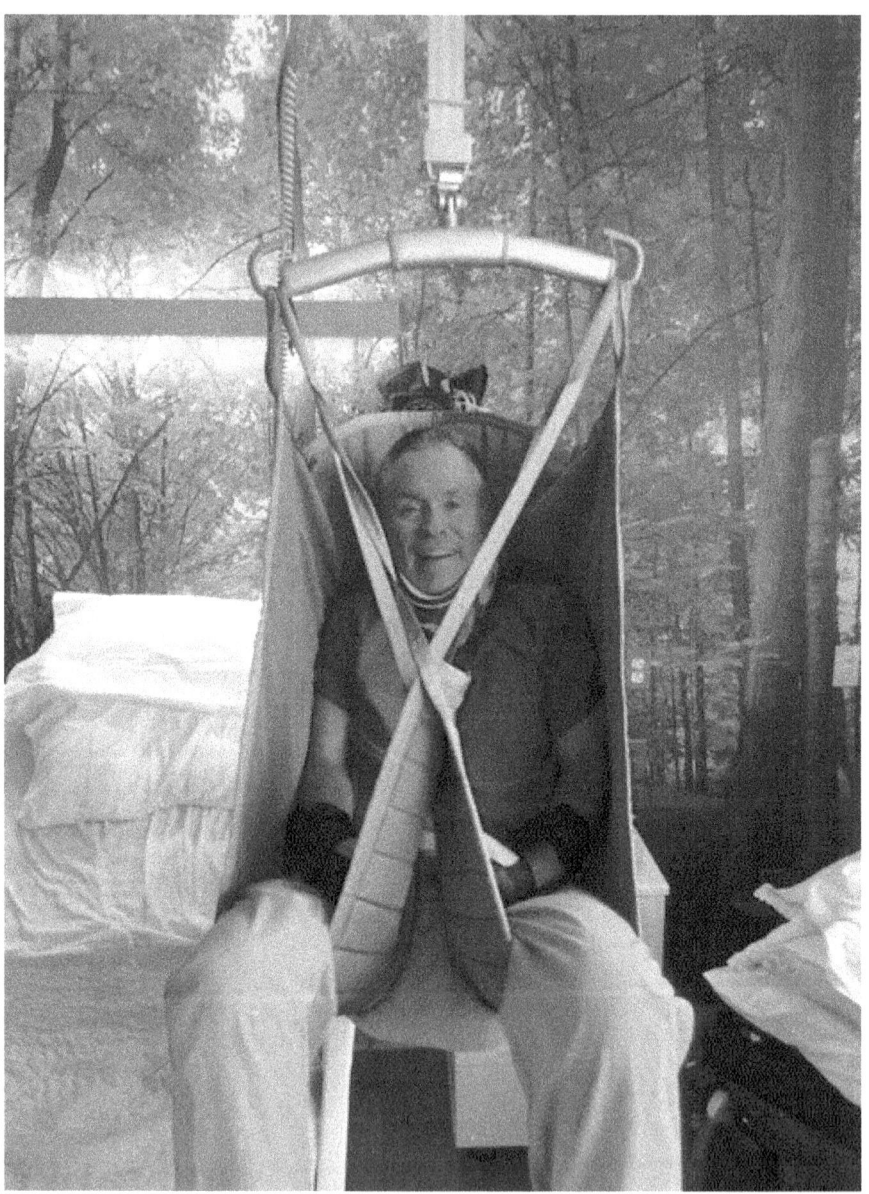

Hanging out in the sling

To further raise my awareness of the dangers of pressure sores, one of my early therapy sessions was spent watching instructional videos about the dangers of pressure sores and how to prevent them. Sarah and my parents were also included as they wanted any and all care takers to also have this knowledge (spoiler alert; I will be telling you more about pressure sores in future chapters). What struck me was the medium in which this message was delivered. The "computer" looked like a first-generation beast. I hadn't seen one of these since before my kids were born. Horrible graphics, terrible puns within the information and it took away from the impact of the message. It made me pause, for just a second, as to how cutting edge this rehab hospital might be. When I inquired, I was told, that the information contained in the old technology was the best available and that there was no reason to swap it out just for purposes of improved graphics.

Another big item of concern presented through these videos, was something called autonomic dysreflexia (AD). AD is a phenomenon that effects those with a spinal cord injury. When AD occurs, there is a sharp increase in blood pressure for no obvious reason. The smallest irritant to my body can cause this. The most common reasons are an issue with the bladder or the bowels. It could be something as simple as a wrinkle in clothing that is pressing on my skin or a hang nail on my toe. The high blood pressure would cause a debilitating headache and a ringing in my ears. The only way to stop an episode is by determining what the irritant is and fixing the issue while raising my head up as high as it will go. AD is so unrecognized by the general medical community that I was given a card to present in any emergency situation to medical personnel with instructions explaining AD and how to correct it. It proved to be beneficial that I had this education as I would have several AD episodes in the future.

Later, in the afternoon, a short Asian man arrived in my room. It was the Chief Medical Officer at MFB, Dr. Ho. He would be my physiatrist during my stay. A physiatrist is a physician that treats medical conditions affecting the brain, spinal cord and nerves. He had been at MFB for over 30 years. Dr. Ho went about explaining what could be expected during my stay. I was comforted as he explained that he and his staff would do everything they could with medicine and therapy to improve my condition. Then he said something that confused me but also gave me comfort. He told us that ultimately my recovery would depend on my willingness to work hard and with the help of a higher power. I had always believed that physicians considered themselves to be Gods and that they didn't necessarily believe in the God I believe in. Rather, they believed more in science. I was very happy to learn that we both knew that God was with us on this journey. Dr. Ho was also a man with a great sense of humor. One of the things he told me that day was that he was confident that I would go home in better shape than I was currently. He told me, "Everyone else go home. I stay."

The final item on my agenda on that first full day was a long-awaited shower. I had no idea how we were going to accomplish this. I had been wearing scrubs moved of the day. One of the techs carefully undressed me while trying not to disturb the tubes attached to me as they moved me around.

For this transfer, I was placed in a different sling and raised by the lift. This new sling was mesh which enabled the water to flow through it as well as to dry quicker. I was lowered by the lift into a very primitive looking "shower chair". This chair was made up of plastic tubing and straps similar to what was used on an old lawn chair. The chair was on wheels. Once I was lowered into it, the slaying was disconnected from the lift but left underneath me. Then I was pushed through the bathroom and into the shower. You'll remember from my earlier description that the bathroom floor was completely flat so rolling me into the shower was not a problem. The shower head was on a handle that could be removed and could reach every part of my body. Again, modesty went out the window as showers were performed by both male and female techs and we just carried on as if everything was normal. My favorite part of every shower was getting my hair shampooed. I've always been a huge fan of having my head rubbed and this was a great way of having this accomplished. The shower was performed in less than 5 minutes. I was pat dried and then wrapped up tightly with additional towels. We then returned to the lift. Another obstacle to overcome was how do you put a wet body into a bed without soaking the sheets? This was solved by placing two large blankets on top of the sheets on my bed. The lift was used to lower me on top of the blankets. After additional pat drying, the blankets were removed from underneath me starting from my head down to my toes. Once I was dry, I was dressed in my pajamas. Wrist braces were placed on each hand. The braces were made of hard plastic and covered with nylon. They were attached to my forearms and wrist with Velcro. The purpose of the wrist braces was to keep my wrists slightly bent. I needed to be able to bend my wrist to help pinch my fingers together. The medical term for this is "tenodesis grasp". Straight, immovable wrists would do me no good. Wraps were placed on my legs from my ankle to my knee. These wraps inflated to help promote blood flow during the night. The wraps were attached to a machine that would inflate and deflate them continuously throughout the night. My wrapped legs were then placed inside plastic boots that were lined with lamb's wool. These boots were to prevent drop foot. These boots kept my toes pointed to the ceiling not allowing them to drop forward.

I soon found out that I would never be able to sleep uninterrupted through the night at MFB. This again, was part of the battle against pressure sores. Twice a night the techs would come in and roll me from one side to the other. I wasn't really rolled completely onto my side. One person would pull me on my side while the other person shoved pillows under my hip and my back. This helped to relieve any pressure I was putting on my backside. This was usually done every four hours. While these tasks were not helpful to my REM sleep, it did provide small windows to chat with the techs about their lives. One of my favorites, from the very beginning, was Hilary, the performer of the quad cough. Hilary was a single mother, who was raising a daughter. We often talked about the challenges she faced and funny stories involving her and her daughter. I think we both got a lot out of those conversations.

When I was healthy, I never gave pooping a second thought. However, I soon found out when you have a spinal cord injury (SCI), pooping becomes an integral part of your routine. My bladder care was under control with the placing of a catheter in my penis. Urine was continuously draining from my bladder without any effort on my part. However, a bowel movement was a participatory activity. One of the early questions I was asked, was prior to the accident, when did I poop? I never thought about that before. My answer was "I pooped when I needed to poop." Apparently, some people have a regular schedule and would go at the same time every day. I was not one of those people. However, I would soon become one at MFB. We determined, just based on my daily schedule, that it would be more convenient for me to be an evening pooper rather than in the morning. The decision was made that I would have a bowel movement every evening, at least for the short term to see how my body would react. Now everything I've previously talked about related to a loss of modesty pales in comparison to the process of having another human engaging in helping you have a bowel movement.

The process began with the insertion of a suppository. This was allowed to "cook" for about 10 minutes so it would take effect. I was raised by the lift, using the same sling we used for showers. Showers were given every other night and the bowel movements were combined with shower times on those days. The same shower chair was used for the pooping process. What I left off of my previous description of the shower chair is the fact that the chair had a hole in the bottom where my butt would hang. Underneath that hole was a plastic bowl to catch anything that might come out of my bowels. At this early stage of my recovery, I had no feeling in my bowels. I could not feel the urge to void my bowels nor could I promote them to void. The tech and I would sit in the bathroom for several minutes to see if the suppository would do its job. If it didn't, I would have to be digitally stimulated by the tech. That process is as horrible as it sounds. Now, it would seem to me, the tech was joining my world of the potential loss of dignity. Amazingly, this never came to fruition. The tech and I just carried on as if this were a normal part of life. What made the job worse for the techs, was the poor design of the shower chair. The tech would have to get down on their hands and knees as I was only 18 inches off the floor. They would awkwardly have to insert their finger in my anus in order to stimulate my bowels. To my surprise, this process worked almost every time. The tech could feel my bowel spasm, remove their finger, and I would poop into the bucket. For the purpose of my charts, the tech would have to rate the volume (small, medium or large) and consistency of my poop. This was the final humiliation of the process. I never examined my poop as closely since becoming a quadriplegic. The biggest lesson I have come away with is that EVERYTHING IS BETTER WHEN YOU POOP!

*Be mentally stronger than
what you feel physically*

—Ray Lewis

CHAPTER 6
My New Normal

Each evening I would receive my schedule of therapy for the following day. When I first arrived, my schedule was to have breakfast around 7:00 A.M. Sarah would feed me my breakfast as I was not yet able to do that on my own. Breakfast would usually consist of a muffin, a fruit cup, and a bowl of cereal. Omelets and pancakes were always offered but I never had a craving for those while at the rehab hospital. A nice perk was that we could order plenty of food for each meal so Sarah was able to get her breakfast through the hospital as well.

After breakfast, my first therapy appointment was with Ashley from OT 8:00 A.M. We spent most of our time stretching my arms. We would also work on daily hygiene tasks such as brushing teeth, washing face, and putting my shirt on. We never tried shaving during these sessions as that had become my Dad's job and he took great pleasure in doing that for me. It was quite a big deal to him to make sure I was clean shaven before he left every evening. Therapy sessions typically lasted 50 minutes.

After my OT, the techs would come in and finish getting me dressed. This consisted of new underwear, sweatpants, putting the ace bandage wraps on my legs, and putting on my shoes. After the first few days, I was able to be transferred into my wheelchair and I would go down to the main gym for my first PT session of the day. The gym was a large room that had several flat tables for patients to work on. The gym contained various pieces of equipment such as, parallel bars, stairs made up of three steps, a tilt table which was used for acclimating patients to being in a standing position (this was similar to the cardiac chair that I used at the hospital in Petoskey). There were several cupboards full of other rehab equipment.

The gym was always a hub of activity. Most days, there were 5 or 6 patients working with their therapists simultaneously. There were regular long tables on the side of the room where patients and therapists could work with various manipulative objects. There was a door to a room that the therapists used for their office. Every activity by every patient had to be documented for internal records as well as for insurance reasons.

As the top of each hour approached, it was quite a mad house as the therapists poured in and out of their office to meet with their patients. At the same time, patience gathered in the gym waiting for their therapist to arrive. The schedule was regimented very effectively. The trains always ran on time at MFB.

Similar to the lift in my room, there was a lift in the gym that was used to move me from my wheelchair to one of the flat tables. These tables were adjustable in height and started off only about two feet off the ground. Initially, I would only use these tables to practice sitting up on the edge. The therapists thought this was an important part of my rehabilitation. All I knew was that I hated it. It was such a simple task but I had a lot of difficulty doing it and it frustrated me. Just being able to sit on a table and not fall over for a couple of seconds was a huge achievement at first. As with most things, I later learned the importance of this small first step.

Following my morning PT session, I would return to my room for lunch. Lunch usually consisted of chicken nuggets and chips. I eventually gravitated to dinosaur shaped chicken nuggets from the kid's menu. There was lots of variety offered on the lunch menu but I always chose the chicken. Again, my parents and Sarah were called on to feed me.

Immediately after lunch, I would have another hour-long session with OT. During this session the therapist would work with my hands to try and coax some sort of movement from them. All of my therapies for the first couple of weeks were very basic, since I couldn't do very much. After OT, I had a second PT session. This session generally consisted of learning how to use my wheelchair. My last session of the day was also a PT session that was just focused on leg stretching. We did this right in my wheelchair and I usually tried to meet the therapist in one of the alcoves which had a large picture window where I could look out onto Grand Rapids.

Therapy generally wrapped up by 4:00 P.M. each day. I was usually pretty exhausted, but at the same time I was always quite exhilarated due to all of the endorphins released during my various exercises. Although the days were long, I always looked forward to tomorrow and to getting more work done. Thankfully, since I did so well on my cognitive test and I was able to eat and speak normally, I did not have to have any speech therapy. That was very welcomed because then I was able to devote that time to rehabbing my body.

The only time that my daily schedule differed was one day a week there was an hour reserved for me to meet with the hospital psychologist. I only met with her for a few weeks before we agreed I had adjusted to my situation quite well and I was keeping an optimistic attitude. I can certainly understand the necessity of counseling time with a psychologist and I was told that I could return to having sessions if I felt I needed them.

Dropping the psychologist meetings from my schedule freed up even more time for OT and PT sessions.

Dinner would arrive close to 5:00 P.M. After dinner, the rest of the evening was spent watching TV, chatting with the nurses and techs and my bowel/shower program. I usually was asleep by 9:00 P.M.

The therapy during the week, was consistent in time and therapists. This was not the case on weekends. The regular therapists were only required to work one weekend day per month. Although my weekend schedule was very light with only 1 or 2 therapy sessions each day, they were always done with various therapists that I did not work with during the week. The weekend schedule for all patients was very light. While many of the patients welcomed this and appreciated the rest, I was always asking for more therapy. After a while, Sarah got to know the scheduler and they would always try to make sure I received therapy on both Saturday and Sunday.

The very first weekend, I was introduced to something that would become a big part of my therapy during my stay at MFB. The first Saturday I was at MFB, a therapist named Jamie, came into my room and announced that we were going to start something called E-Stim. E-stim stood for electronic stimulation. Initially, I was hesitant because the only electronic stimulation I was familiar with was used on patients in an insane asylum. I was picturing Jack Nicholson in "One Flew Over the Cuckoo's Nest".

The e-stim was explained to me as a tool to bridge the gap between my brain and the rest of my body. Since my spinal cord accident, my brain could no longer communicate with other parts of my body to get them to move. By placing electrodes on my arms and sending an electrical charge to them my arms and hands could move as if my brain was communicating with them.

Placing the electrodes in different parts of my body would control the movement of different parts of my body. I could feel the charge through my skin coming from the electrodes. With Sarah, Andy, Alyson and my parents all witnessing this at my bedside, I was able to lift my arm up off the bed and move it around. I wasn't in control of the movement, but it was an awesome sight to see my arm move like it used to move. It was pretty emotional for all of us and I was ecstatic. Here it was our "light" weekend therapy day and this was the greatest thing I had seen in my five days at MFB so far. Unfortunately, we were only able to do this for an hour but he moved the electrodes around and I was able to move my hands and my fingers as well. I knew it was possible for them to move. This one activity was able to raise my optimism to a new level!

My parents were at the hospital during therapy times and meal times, for the first few months. They were able to stay nearby at a small bed and breakfast styled house called "Sophia's Place". This was about a 5-minute walk from the hospital. Sophia's Place was affiliated with several of the hospitals in the area and provided comfortable, low-cost lodging for families of patients. My parents loved it. Sophia's had a community kitchen where food had been brought in either through the families staying there or outside donors that was available to all of guests. This was a great convenience and eased a bit of stress for them.

Each Wednesday, meetings were held regarding the progress of every patient. These meetings were generally quick, 5-10 minutes in length. In attendance at each meeting was Dr. Ho, each of my therapists, the nurse that was working with me that day and a representative from my insurance company. The main purpose of these meetings was to update my progress and to determine how long I would need to stay at the rehab hospital. This was critical so that all of the necessary paperwork was completed properly with appropriate documentation to continue my time at MFB. My initial meeting set my date of release for 10 weeks. This was approximately the first week of October. As I would find out later, the date of discharge was very fluid.

I took meds four times a day. The greatest bulk of the medication was given in the morning. I was on 4 different medications for muscle relaxation. One of the biggest things I fight each day as a spinal cord injury patient are muscle spasms and a tightening of the muscles called "tone". The muscle spasms are just random movement of my arms and legs that would normally be very painful but I could not feel them. All I saw was the results of my arms and legs moving without any control. Muscle tone refers to a muscle wanting to go in one direction all of the time. For example, my leg would often times straighten so it was difficult for me to bend that leg on command. I didn't start my recovery with four different muscle relaxers but as we reached the maximum dose on one medication, Dr. Ho would add another medication. I also took medicine to help with my digestive system. These were simple over the counter things like Metamucil, Pepcid and assorted probiotics. I also received a heparin shot each morning in my stomach. This was to prevent any type of blood clots to form. I could never feel the injection but I always looked forward to the day that I would. I also took Lexapro for anxiety, something I had never had to deal with before the accident.

Obviously, I had been through quite a traumatic incident. While, I always thought I kept a positive attitude and projected that outwardly, occasionally I would have my doubts internally. Anxiety is not something I was familiar with. Until this accident I had no idea what a panic attack or extreme anxiety felt like. On a few occasions, I would find it difficult to catch my breath and my mind was thinking of things way too fast. I didn't understand why my body and mind were failing me. Sarah would ask the nurse to give me a Xanax, as had been prescribed on an as needed basis, and within a few minutes I would find it easier to breath and I could feel myself calming down. If you ever suffer panic attacks ask your doctor about Xanax, I would recommend it and I'm not even a paid spokesman. I still take Xanax as a muscle relaxer to this day whenever I get tight enough that I am prevented from completing my daily tasks. I almost never have anxiety. I believe that is because I have already experienced such a terrible trauma and I think, "What's the worst thing that could happen? I'm already paralyzed."

An important thing for any patient to remember is that you are your best advocate! Nobody else knows what you are going through or knows exactly what you need at a given time. The staff at MFB was very open to communication back and forth. It was also much easier since Sarah was included in every conversation and knew what was going on. She was able to advocate for me as well. No patient should just sit back and accept any and all medical treatment without an understanding of what is being done. Prior to my accident, I had little experience with self-advocating or very little contact with the medical profession. I would avoid hospitals at all cost. I even hated to visit anyone in the hospital. However, advocacy is something I learned and cannot stress enough how vital it is to make your recovery more successful. Every time I received medicine, the nurse would tell me what I was taking and what it was for. Every time we tried a new exercise in therapy, I would ask for an explanation of what were we trying to accomplish. This not only made me feel better, by having the knowledge, but it also pleased the medical staff that I was engaged in my care.

Meanwhile, outside of the hospital, Sarah and I had been scheduled to move out of our apartment and into a condo in Fenton, MI. This move was to have taken place two days after my accident. Since Sarah and I were fully engaged in my care, the burden of rescheduling our move fell upon Andy. Andy's first step was to reschedule the movers for another day. We still had to be out of the apartment in two weeks. How were we going to pull that off? This is where an extensive network of family and friends really came through for us. Through social media, Andy was able to contact my Griswold buddies, other friends as well as our family members and the response was overwhelming! We had all kinds of volunteers willing to step up and help us out. I had moved several loads of boxes to the condo prior to the golf trip, but there was still all of the furniture and where to put things in the condo that needed to be addressed. On the last Saturday in August, many of our friends and family members were able to move everything out of the apartment and into the condo without any problems. We will always be grateful to everyone who participated and took this big worry off our plate.

One of the Griswolds that I mentioned earlier, Bob Chapman, is a very well-connected person. We always joked that "Chappy has a guy". It didn't matter what it was, Chappy had a source that could help. Taking inspiration from the Live Strong yellow, rubber bracelets that Lance Armstrong sold to raise money for cancer research, Chappy and his wife, Julie, came up with a bracelet to unite all of my friends and to ensure that I stayed in their thoughts and prayers. Bob knew a guy that produced those type of bracelets. Bob and Julie paid for 250 red bracelets imprinted with "We're All In". Soon, everyone I knew was wearing one of those bracelets. Even the staff at MFB were wearing them. Demand became so strong back home in Grand Blanc, that Sarah bought a another 600 to distribute to students and staff in the schools. Later there was another order of 250. I still wear mine and I still see others with them on as well. The Chapmans are a powerful duo and I am grateful for everything they did and continue to do for Sarah and I.

Once again, Sarah and I were amazed by the outpouring of support. It mattered! Knowing that many people cared helped to give me more strength every day. I didn't want to let any of them down by giving less than 100%. Sarah had always told me that making connections with people was important. I never gave that much thought until witnessing all of the support we received after my accident.

Recovery is not a race.
Do not feel guilty if it takes longer than
you thought it would

—Unknown

CHAPTER 7
The MFB Team

As I mentioned earlier, the unsung heroes at MFB are the nurse techs. I dealt with several of them each day. We shared a lot of stories. For example, have you ever been prayed for in Swahili? Well, I have. Mambo did that for me. She was a refugee from the Congo. One night she came into my room, leaned over my head, closed her eyes and began whispering. I wasn't sure what was going on but I laid there quietly and let her do her thing. I didn't recognize the language but it definitely wasn't English. She eventually raised her head looked at me and shared that she had prayed for me in Swahili. I felt a sense of peace. I was blessed to have many positive interactions with Mambo during my time at MFB. Always smiling, she had a great laugh. She worked hard and always made me feel that she cared about me. I know she made me feel special in all of our contacts. To this day, we still keep in touch through Facebook.

Troy was another tech that I spent a lot of time with. He was always going a million miles per hour in a million different directions. He was always thinking about what he could do to make the hospital an even better place for the patients and their families. He stopped by often even if he wasn't my assigned tech. He would bounce his latest idea off of me to see what I thought. If Troy had a specialty, it was the dreaded bowel program. He was always trying to perfect a technique and share it with his colleagues. I always referred to him as the hardest working man at Mary Free Bed. Regardless whether he actually was or not, he certainly made it look that way. Always breathing hard and perspiring. He was one of the oldest techs on staff. He loved telling stories and listening to mine. He still works at MFB and we keep in touch through Facebook as well.

On the other end of the spectrum was Matt. He was a youngster and full of energy. This job was a good income source as he prepared to move on to bigger and better things. He was planning to go to nursing school. Matt had a good relationship with one of my nurses, Catherine. They were very entertaining, including a shaving cream fight one evening. Other techs that I spent a lot of time with included Brandon and Ashleigh. They often worked the same shift and flirted so outwardly that I finally told them to end the charade and start dating. Ashleigh smiled slyly and told me that they had already tried that. Matt's story did not have a happy ending. For reasons unknown to me, he committed suicide. On the outside, he seemed to be very happy but obviously he was battling some type of demon.

As you go through life remember that you never know what a person is dealing with. We should all keep in mind that you never know what issues people may be working through and we should always be kind to each other. This is another one of the many life lessons Sarah has taught me. When a car speeds past us, we'll look at each other and one of us will comment "they must be late for dialysis."

Without a doubt, the person I enjoyed the most was a tech named Becca. She and I clicked immediately as she was as much of a smartass as me. We exchanged snarky comments nonstop. An outsider might have thought we didn't get along. We could both dish it out and take it. It made both of us happy to be in each other's lives. Becca's favorite way to get under my skin was to throw my dirty underwear on my face when undressing me at night. The techs were all a lot of fun to work with and were the heart of MFB.

September 22nd was my 52nd birthday. Of course, I spent it at MFB. Sarah knew this would be hard on me. In another demonstration of Sarah's connections to so many people, she put out a request to anyone that knew me to send me a card. MFB had an internal system to deliver patient mail to their rooms. They must've hated us for a period of time. The gentleman that delivered the mail each day always made a comment about how much mail I was getting. He attempted to keep a count, but gave up after a while. We estimated the number to be several hundred! The number of cards pouring in made me feel so loved. If you ever doubted that some small seemingly insignificant thing that you do for another person doesn't mean anything, please put that thought out of your head. Laying on the bed with all those cards spread over me is one of the lasting images I have of this entire journey. It brought tears to my eyes. Being kind to others matters. Sarah has been trying to teach me that for over 30 years.

The entire journey has taught me so much about the connections that Sarah has always preached to me about. I usually rolled my eyes at her because I had heard so many stories from her about connections. As wives usually are, Sarah was correct about this as well. My tragic accident had brought so many people back into my life. Obviously, I wish I could've done it another way, but having more people in my life and knowing that they cared so much made things a little bit easier. As I said about the birthday cards, always remember that no gesture you make towards another person is too small. They all matter. Love one another!

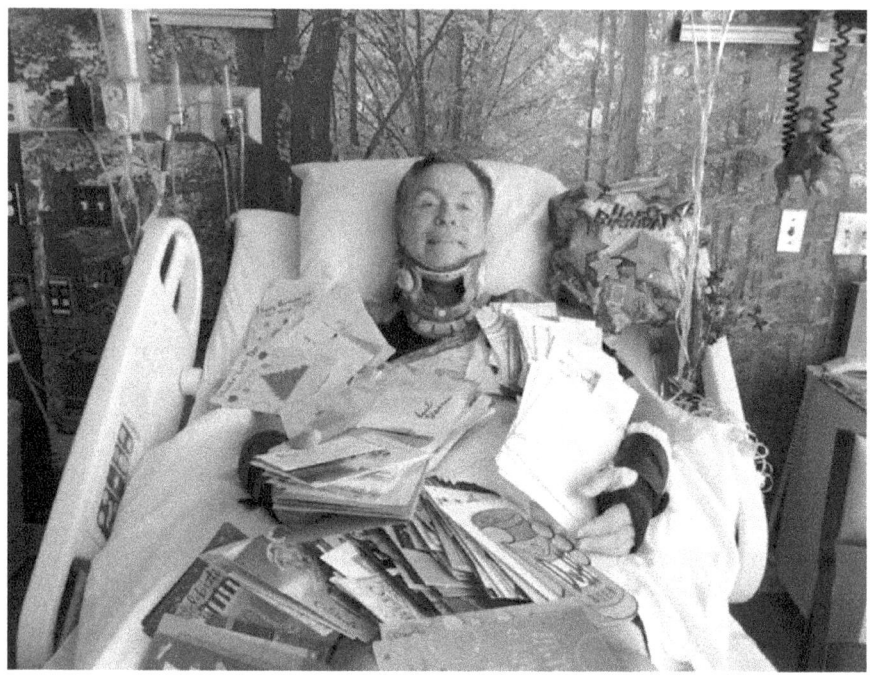

My Birthday Cards

One of my favorite re-connections that has occurred was with my college roommate George. We had never met until freshman move-in day at Central Michigan University. We had so many similar interests, baseball being the primary one, that we became close friends immediately. George was my best man at my wedding and likewise I was his. Years passed, children were raised and our contact dwindled. He visited me on a few occasions at MFB but his greatest contribution was sending me trivia questions at least once a week. He sent these through the mail. Unheard of, right? He was especially proud of the various stamps he would purposely pick out at the post office. George is an old soul. They went a long way in lifting my spirits. Now we fire emails back and forth several times a week. We even did a podcast during the Covid years. Please check it out: "George and Keith's Musings". You can find it on any of the podcast platforms. I guarantee you will learn at least one thing from every podcast!

A week after my birthday, Sarah and I took our first field trip off the hospital grounds. We went with a handful of other patients and therapists to a huge outdoor celebration in Grand Rapids called Art Prize. Art Prize was an opportunity for local artists to display their talents - maybe even make a little money. I had never heard of it before, but it was very well attended. We took a small bus to the event. It was my first opportunity to roll onto a ramp and then be lifted up into the van. I was moved to a part of the bus in which there were hooks embedded in the floor. Straps were then attached to my wheelchair and to the hooks on the floor. This locked me into position so that I would not move around in the bus. Normally, I would think nothing of moving from display to display working my way through the crowds. However, I had never done this before in a wheelchair. So many new experiences. Maneuvering my way through narrow spaces. Finding ramps so that I could go up on the sidewalk to experience the next exhibit. The toughest challenge by far was avoiding people. The majority of people were very kind and provided me a wide berth to pass. However, Art Prize is a very visual experience. People weren't always looking where they were going. I understand that now in hindsight, but I was very frustrated at the time. The obliviousness of so many people. Each of them not knowing how close they were to getting their foot run over by a 500-pound wheelchair. We survived and there were no casualties. It was a successful first day in the "real world".

During my stay at Mary Free Bed, the most important group of people for my physical recovery were the therapists. My physical therapy (PT) team was led by two women both of whom were much stronger than they looked. Laura and Tracy were both doctors of physical therapy. They job shared, so while I rarely saw them together, I always saw one of them each weekday. Both were accepting of my quirky sense of humor and I'm pretty sure they always got the joke. They rarely fired back with a comment of their own, but when they did, it was well worth the wait.

As I mentioned earlier, the first Few weeks of OT were pretty uneventful as I was able to do very little. Lots of sitting on the edge of the mat table to work on my balance and core strength. I was assured that I was doing a good job although it was difficult for me to tell. Eventually, I could sit up for several minutes at a time without wobbling over.

Other tasks we would undertake would be lying on my back on the mat and trying to move my legs out to the sides. They would make it a little bit easier on me by putting a trash bag like pad under my foot to reduce the friction. I required a lot of help with those but we needed to do them to prevent atrophy setting in from just sitting idly all day. Driving the wheelchair also fell under the responsibilities of the PT team.

The third member of the PT team was also named Tracey. She was actually a physical therapist assistant. She had less formal education in PT than Laura or Tracy, but she did not lack for practical education or work ethic. She was the smallest member of the team, but she could hold her own when it came to throwing me around. As time went on, I gave her the name "Good Luck Tracey" (GLT). She always seemed to be on the scene when I would set a new record in whatever we happened to be working on that day. It didn't hurt that it helped to differentiate between Tracy/Tracey as well.

Additionally, I had the bonus of a student working with me as well. Her name was Kara. She was a student at Central Michigan University and a pitcher on their softball team. We had plenty to talk about since we were both CMU graduates (Fire Up Chips!). I peppered her with questions about various campus buildings and how they were holding up. Her 6-foot frame was no doubt helpful when pitching and also as a PT. It was always good to have another set of hands around when I started to struggle during one of our exercises. As she gained experience, Laura or

Tracy gave her more time working with me as the lead therapist. She fit right in and did a great job.

One thing I learned early on is that therapists can't count. I don't know if they do it on purpose or not but I am always certain to count the repetitions of an exercise we are doing on my own because if I didn't, 10 reps became 12 or 15. That was true from my first day and is still true today during my outpatient therapy visits.

In They may not be able to count but all the therapists I have worked with during the past 10 years are very personable. Therapists need to be extroverts. Working together in such close quarters would be much more difficult if done in silence. I can only imagine how much more difficult it would be for them when working with an uncooperative patient. I always keep that in mind even when I am having a bad day.

My occupational therapy with Ashley started to move away from stretching and more towards strengthening. I spent a lot of time on an arm bike. The arm bike was set up so that I could pull my wheelchair right up to the machine. Since I didn't have much arm strength in the beginning, electrodes were attached to my arms from my wrists to my shoulders to fire the muscles. The electrodes were secured to my arms by an ace bandage with a small opening at my elbow so I could bend it. We had an hour scheduled for my sessions but a good part of that time was spent attaching and then detaching the electrodes. After noticing how much therapy time I was missing out on, Sarah asked Ashley to teach her how to set me up on the arm bike. Ashley agreed to teach her and within a short while my wife, the unofficial physical therapy assistant, became quite proficient in attaching the electrodes which cut our set up time almost in half. Soon we became even more clever and arrived at the bike early. If it was unoccupied, Sarah would start prepping me so that we would be ready to go when Ashley arrived. As time passed and I got stronger, the amount of the electrical charge was reduced so my muscles were doing more of the work.

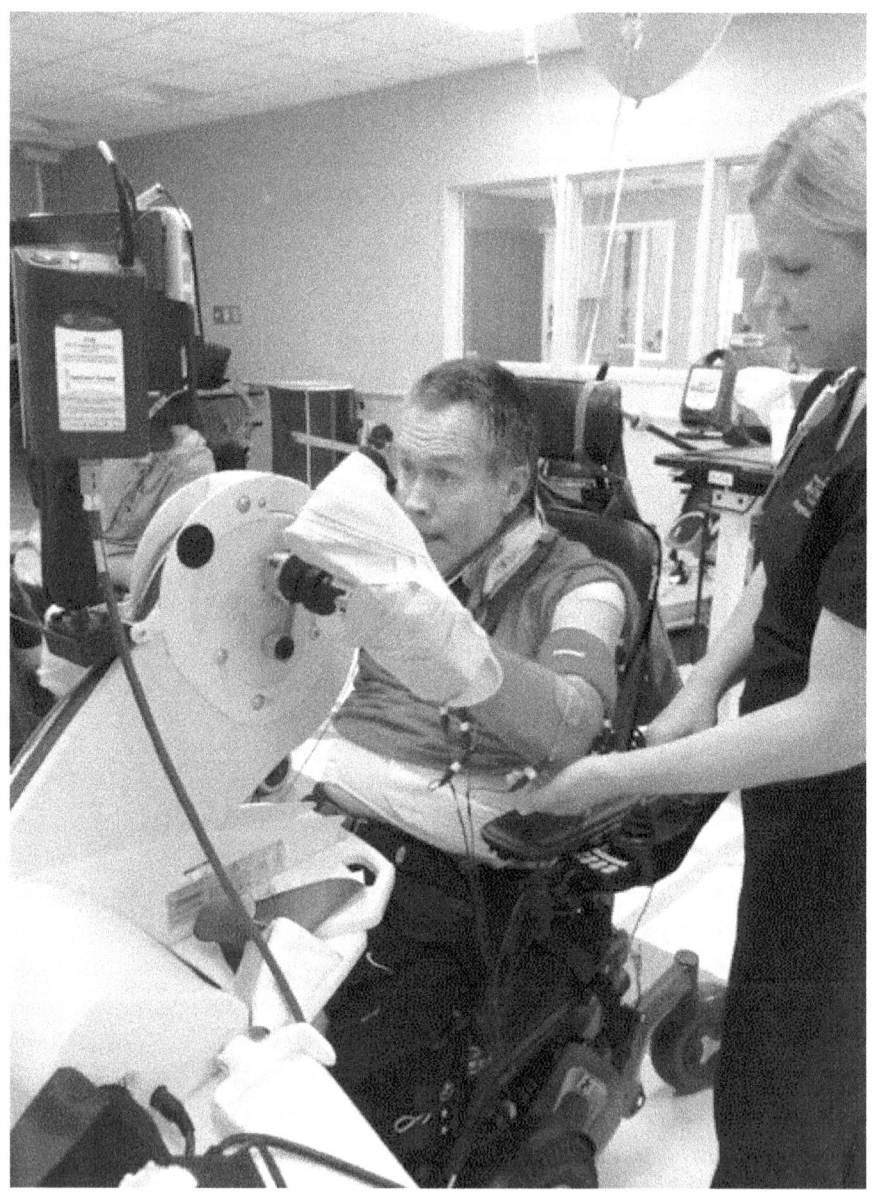

On The Arm Bike With My OT, Ashley

As I told you earlier, I had a catheter that went directly into my penis and my urine flowed directly into a Foley bag. The bag generally fills up two or three times a day. Urine production was considered healthy, so I was encouraged to drink as much as possible. The problem with an external catheter is that it left me more susceptible to urinary tract infections (UTI). An option for a lot of paralyzed people is to self-catheterize. In other words, when they felt the urge to urinate, they would insert a tube through their penis into their bladder and drain the urine as needed. It was decided that it was unlikely that I would get the manipulation back in my fingers to be able to do that. The answer to my problem was something called a suprapubic catheter (SP). An SP is a catheter surgically placed inside the bladder. This reduced the number of UTIs while simultaneously not requiring self-catheterization. UTIs are nasty. My thoughts get very cloudy and I sometimes have hallucinations. I was anxious to avoid UTIs at almost any cost. The surgery took place on October 8 without complication and I was allowed to return to MFB that same day. My urine still drains into a Foley bag that needs to be emptied just as it was before. At bedtime, a larger bag is connected to my SP tube so that it doesn't need to be changed during the night. One of the nurses, Leslie, made a cloth bag to discreetly store my Foley bag so I could wear shorts without anyone having to look at my unappealing bag of urine.

Earlier I wrote about AD headaches that bring with them extremely high blood pressure and painful headaches. Having a problem with the bladder is one of the most common triggers for an AD episode. When this has happened to me in the past it is usually due to a kink in the tube leading to my Foley bag. If the kink prevents urine from flowing into the Foley bag the urine backs up into my bladder until it is beyond capacity. Other times, Sarah and I forget to attach the night bag and my smaller capacity leg bag fills leaving the urine with no place to go except back to my bladder. Once the leg bag is emptied the urine in my bladder flows into the leg bag and the headache goes away as fast as it came on. I still have the SP in place today and will for the rest of my life. Congratulations, dear reader. By my count urine or urinary was used 11 times in the last three paragraphs. You won't beat that record reading books by John Grisham, Stephen King or JK Rowling. You're welcome!

I didn't know where my shoes ended up after the accident but I wanted something to wear on my feet when I was in the wheelchair. It certainly wasn't an issue of comfort for me, obviously, because I couldn't feel my feet or the foot plates of the wheelchair. It was explained to us, however, that even though I couldn't feel the shoes, a good fit was important so that I did not irritate my feet or cause any sores. It wasn't like I could head out to the mall and pick out some shoes myself. I asked Sarah to go out and buy me the "cheapest shoes she could find". Since I wasn't going to be walking in them, I didn't want to spend a lot of money on comfort. She returned with the ugliest pair of tennis shoes I had ever seen. They were plain black with Velcro straps. Even my six-year-old great niece, Adelynn, could see how hideous they were. Rather than mocking me she did something about it. She took my shoes and came back a short time later with a gorgeous pair of "bedazzled" shoes. Multicolored and sparkly, I was proud to accept the compliments that came from all those who saw them. I was happy to tell my story about Adelynn's ingenuity.

Always focus on how far you have come, not how far you have to go

—Rick Warren

CHAPTER 8
Big Changes

Each night when I couldn't go immediately back to sleep after being turned by the techs, I attempted to get my brain to connect with my body. I would try to move my fingers in the outline of the alphabet. I was hoping this would somehow send a message to my brain as to how they should be moving. I did the same thing with my big toe. I did this night after night for weeks. Temporarily disheartened by failure but never to the point where I quit. No one told me to do this. I was just hopeful.

I'll never forget the date, October 13, 2015. Per usual, I started with my index fingers. No luck. Next, I tried my right big toe. Something felt different. I could swear it was moving but it was 2:30 in the morning, the room was dark and my feet were covered with blankets so I couldn't see them. Sarah was sleeping soundly and I didn't want to bother her with what was most likely a false alarm. Nonetheless, I continued on. I switched to my left big toe. I had the same feeling of movement. Then I tried wiggling all of my toes. Success! I continued moving my toes for quite a while. I laid there in the dark wishing there was a way I could prove to myself that it was actually happening and it wasn't just a dream.

Next, I tried moving my legs from side to side like I had done with help during therapy. I was doing it! I returned to moving my toes just to make sure that was still real. They were still movable! I started to tear up and was unable to wipe them away. The salt from my tears stung for a while but it was really the best feeling in the world.

I tried to bend my legs at the knees and drag my heal up towards my butt. That was not happening. The next thing I did was attempt to squeeze my buttocks. This was working! My mind was racing. I was certain I was awake. This couldn't be a dream.

I kept doing these exercises for the next three hours still not 100% believing what I was feeling and hesitant to wake up Sarah. Finally, 6 o'clock arrived which was close enough to our normal wake up time that I called out her name. I asked Sarah to put her hand under my left buttock. Sarah just stared at me and replied "I'm not doing that!" Under any circumstance, a sane person would be skeptical of such a request. Sarah's skepticism was even greater because we had had a recent conversation about how much I wished I could have an audible fart. It had been nothing but silent gas for me. She had to be thinking I had rediscovered my ability to fart in tune. Regardless, with a little more prodding, my lovely bride, placed her hand under the covers and cupped my butt. I squeezed and I felt the same sensation that I had felt during the night. One look at her face told me that she felt it as well. This was really happening!

I asked her to remove the blankets and turn on the lights. She and I were able to see my toes move for the first time in almost 2 months. Another miracle! I'm losing track... Is that four? Even the most hopeful stories I had heard from other patients was the movement of a single toe. The movement I was getting was unbelievable. Sarah and I had a lot of thankful discussions with God that morning. He had come through for us once again! We hugged and cried a lot. My optimism had always been high, but now it was through the roof. Everything was coming together.

My hard work, my faith in God, the love of my wife and my optimistic attitude all working together to create a miracle!

I couldn't wait to share the news with anyone and everyone. Even though it was so early in the morning we called my parents and then our boys. I am sure receiving a call from Sarah's phone at that early hour caused a moment of dread for each of them. Who calls with good news that early? We made sure to remove any fears they might have regarding the call and I immediately told them about my newly discovered movement. Each response was similar. Disbelieving silence at first. Followed by clarification that they were hearing correctly. Finally, tears of thankfulness. We didn't know what this development meant but obviously it was a fantastic turning point in my life!

The first people I see in the morning are the techs that get me dressed and ready for the day. As each new person entered my room, I was more than happy to show them my new abilities. The MFB team was like a family to me, so as I showed each person what I could do, there was a brand-new squeal of excitement. Some crying, but always smiling and happy. It was so uplifting to Sarah and I to see how excited they were about something that was so important to us. As word spread, we had dozens of visitors stop by with good wishes, even staff members I had never worked with before. Just another reason why the experience at MFB is second to none.

I hadn't seen Becca yet. I really wanted to tell Becca! I don't recall if she was working later that day or if she didn't see me for an entire day, but I wanted to keep her in the dark and show her my new movement in a unique way. When I finally saw her, I was in my wheelchair. I asked Becca to bend down and see if I had something on my shoe. As she was hovering over my foot, I used every ounce of strength I had to lift my leg and lightly kick her in the nose. She looked at me and all she could do was laugh. I think I even saw a tear in the eye of tough ol' Becca.

This development caused a dramatic change in my therapies and in my length of stay. I had no idea how this improvement would change the direction of my therapy. At the next insurance meeting, my release date was extended to December 9. The intensity and focus of my therapies were ratcheted up considerably. I had wiggled my toes on October 13th and by October 15th I was introduced to a new piece of equipment called the Lokomat.

Due to the remodeling being done at the hospital, the Lokomat was temporarily stored in a dark uninhabited part of the hospital. I had never discussed the Lokomat with any of my therapists. I'm certain the reason was because nobody expected me to progress this far. The Lokomat was a treadmill on steroids. A harness was wrapped around my waist as I sat in my wheelchair. Additional straps crisscrossed my inner thighs. The straps connected to a hydraulic lift that enabled the amount of weight I carried to be adjusted. I wore gloves with Velcro straps to attach my hands to posts that were waist high just in front of me.

With concerns of my blood pressure on the therapist's minds the signal was given to raise me to a standing position. The straps were extremely tight. This tightness was supposed to help with the flow of blood to minimize low blood pressure issues. Even though I was still wearing my neck collar, those muscles had atrophied to the point where I could not lift my head up. An additional strap was wrapped around my forehead and attached to the back of the harness to keep my head upright.

The parts of the Lokomat that made it stand out and look so futuristic were the hydraulic pieces that attached to the sides of my legs. They looked like something right out of the Robocop movie. Made of hard plastic and steel, the hydraulics moved my legs at the hips and knees.

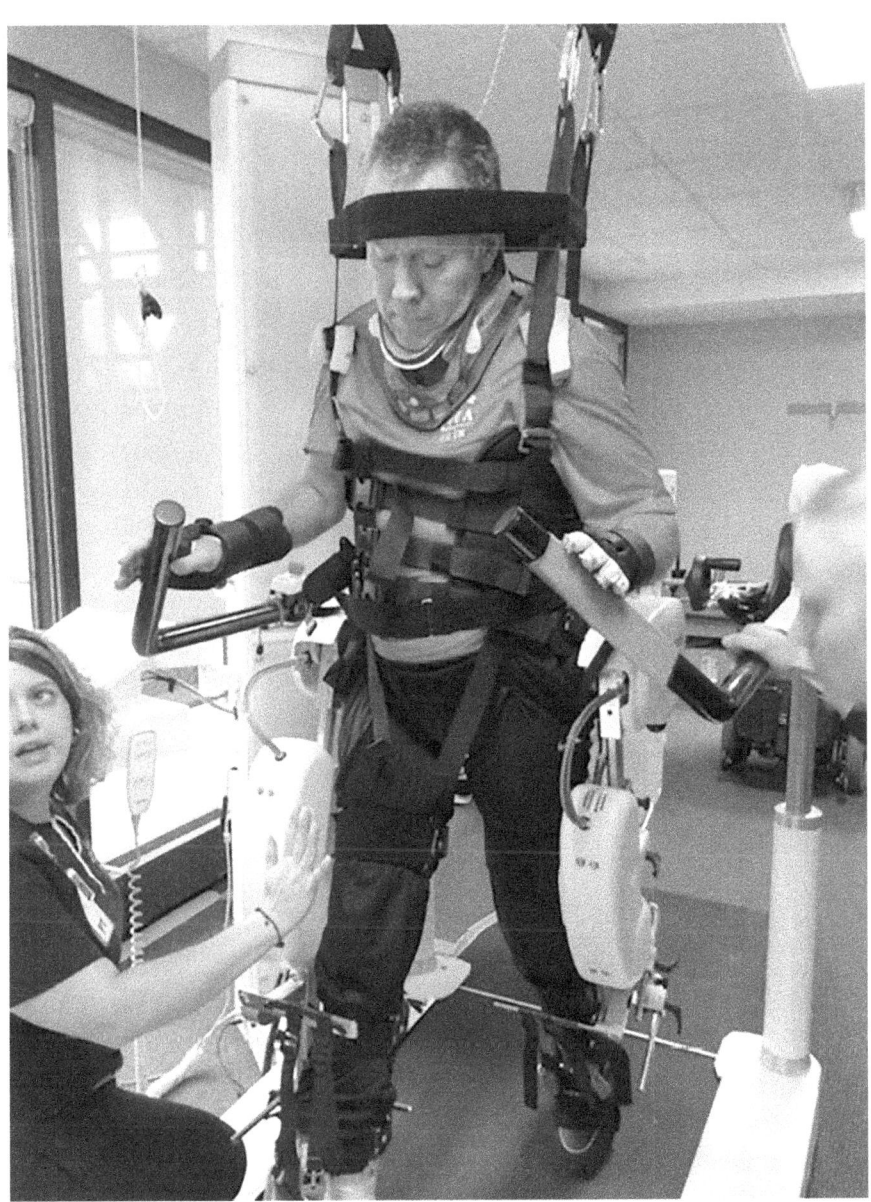

The Lokomat

Set up was quite time-consuming. I was very anxious that first day. Happy to be on my feet but nervous about the unknown. The Lokomat was switched on and the treadmill began to move slowly. I could feel the hydraulics beginning to move my legs. An unbelievable sensation that only three days ago I never would have thought possible. A full-length mirror was placed in front of me so I could see for myself what my body was doing. Even though I had the robotic legs helping to propel me, the therapists had to kneel on either side of me and manually help push my legs forward as well. I felt like a ragdoll as I hung there and tried so hard to keep my legs moving. Regardless, it was an unbelievable sensation. Only three days ago I would've never thought this would be possible. Now there was a chance that I would walk again! My optimism had never been higher. Although, I had no idea what an acceptable time was to "walk" during my first day on the Lokomat I was able to move productively for 18 minutes and 41 seconds. I always had Sarah keep track of my results on all of the equipment. My goal was to set a new record each time.

As I progressed on the Lokomat things were made more difficult. The therapists placed pieces of foam rubber about 2 inches high on the treadmill. This forced me to lift my leg higher than I had been. The Lokomat became my primary PT activity. After working on this piece of equipment 3 to 5 times a week for a month I "graduated" to the next phase of walking.

Next up to continue my walking progression was a contraption called "Zero Gravity". The zero gravity still involved a harness and the ability to reduce some of the body weight that I would normally have to carry on my own. However, instead of walking on a treadmill I walked across the floor. The Zero Gravity was located on the fourth floor. It wasn't nearly as futuristic looking as the Lokomat. However, it was more realistic since I was walking across the floor. This machine was operated by the therapists through a series of ropes. The ropes operated the harnesses which were used to adjust the amount of weight I carried on my own. There was a metal track embedded in the ceiling that held the harness that followed me as I worked my way down the hallway. My first day I was able to support 115 pounds of my own weight. I was getting stronger every day! For several weeks, I rotated between using the Lokomat and the Zero Gravity.

Another new activity I was exposed to, was spending time in the pool. The pool was supposed to have been closed weeks ago due to renovations at the hospital. However, delays kept pushing that closing date back. God had intervened on my behalf again. Being in the pool reduces body weight, which would allow for better mobility without all the restrictions of harnesses and electronics. I walked the width of the pool with the aid of Diane, who performed all kinds of PT duties, but in fact she became my de facto personal pool therapist. I had flotation devices on my arms and neck to keep me buoyant. The lower effect of gravity made walking much easier. As time went on, I was able to increase the number of times I walked back and forth. Each pool session ended in my favorite part of being in the pool, with a relaxation technique called "Bad Ragaz". Diane told me it was developed in Switzerland in the 1930s. All I had to do was lay on my back and close my eyes. She would grab my legs and just slowly pull me through the pool letting the water wash over me. I feel relaxed just thinking about it,

I did have some concerns about using the pool. I always feared having a bowel movement. If that were to happen, the pool would have had to have been drained and cleaned. This would keep everybody out of the pool for several days. My mind flashed back to the movie "Caddyshack" and the scene in which Carl, in full hazmat suit had to clean the pool after such an incident. I can probably report that my fears were unnecessary and I never caused a shutdown. I got into the pool once or twice a week until it finally did close in December.

Relaxing In The Pool

Major events occurred in November! Due to my progress walking, my release day was extended another four weeks. On November 8, after 12 weeks, my neck brace was finally removed. Yikes! Talk about a neck beard. My dad would have had a field day shaving that but he was back home in Florida and missed his great opportunity. Carmela's friend Marilyn came to my rescue and cleaned me up. It was so much more comfortable being rid of that brace. The next day, at long last, audible farts returned to my repertoire. No one else seemed as pleased as I was.

The following week I took delivery on two of the most expensive pieces of equipment I had ever possessed. First, came my Permobil 3 power wheelchair. You might think it to be strange that I was excited about a wheelchair in which I would spend the huge majority of my time for the rest of my life, but denying that fact wasn't going to change a thing.

The wheelchair came equipped with a special cushion called a Roho. This cushion contained several air-filled columns to help prevent pressure sores on my bottom. Pressure sores are basically open, ugly breakthroughs on my skin that can easily get infected. (Do you remember the old-time movie they showed me when I first arrived at MFB?) The wheelchair had a T-bar handle for a joystick. This enabled my hand to easily control the wheelchair. It had two levels of speed with five additional settings of speed within each level. Level I, setting 1 was very, very slow - it was appropriate for a beginner. Level II, setting 5 was dangerously fast and it would be a while for me to become expert enough to attempt that speed.

The wheelchair also had several different positional adjustments. There was an elevator mode that can be used to raise the entire seat about 18 inches. This is useful when sitting at a high-top table. Also, the entire chair tipped back. This is most important for the previously mentioned pressure relief. The back of the chair also moves back independently. This was useful to me to stretch my hips. I also needed to get into a flat position for some of the therapy sessions when I didn't transfer out of the wheelchair. The final movement enabled the foot plates to be raised. This is also a good stretch for me. The insurance company has determined that the life expectancy of a power wheelchair is about five years.

The other big-ticket delivery was our modified Chrysler Town & Country van. The passenger side sliding door opened and a ramp extended outward. The ramp is about 6 feet long and folds in half when it is stored in the van. You might have noticed additional room between some of the handicap parking spots that indicate van parking only. My type of van with a side ramp is what those signs are referring to. I needed the extra space so there was enough room for the ramp to deploy and so that I could safely exit the van. The ramp is about one foot wider than my wheelchair. There is a three-inch lip that helps to keep my wheelchair on the ramp in case it went astray. I have had a couple of close calls but I have always kept the wheelchair upright. Although, I have given Sarah a few scares through the years.

The van also has a system of hydraulics that lowers height of the van when the ramp is deployed. Other than that, it is like any other van with a power sliding door on the driver's side and a liftgate at the rear.

Please, please pay attention to the blue handicap parking spots and the striped areas adjacent to them. For some time, I have wanted to make signs reading "Please park better next time" and place them on the scofflaw's windshield. Sarah pointed out, correctly, that there are a lot of crazy people out there that would think nothing of physically attacking us or our vehicle because of it. As demonstrated by the pictures below you can see why Sarah and I are continually amazed by an individual's inability to park properly. Recently I found out about an app called "Parking Mobility". By submitting a picture of the front and rear of the offending vehicle, including a license plate number, the fine folks at Parking Mobility can send a not so friendly reminder to the offending party. Do it as a favor for handicapped people everywhere, including your old pal, Keith.

The most common way to secure the wheelchair in the van is through the use of straps and hooks that attach to the floor of the van. While we have that option, our van is equipped with a special aftermarket docking station. My wheelchair is equipped with a post that is attached to the bottom of the wheelchair. I pull my wheelchair into that docking station where the front passenger would normally sit. The original front passenger seat has been removed from the van. When properly lined up, the wheelchair post locks in to the docking station. This is much more convenient than having to manually secure the chair with four straps and a seatbelt.

The post is not without some problems however. My ground clearance is lessened by that post. Occasionally, I get hung up on a high threshold. Also, properly lining up the wheelchair post with the docking station proved to be quite an undertaking. Especially at first, when I had no sense of where I needed to be in order to successfully complete the task. It sometimes takes several attempts before I succeed. Even some of those can be rough. I will feel the chair hang up on the docking station because it isn't perfectly lined up, but I stubbornly refuse to start over only to eventually slam quite violently into the locked position. Sarah does not find this amusing. Now after doing it hundreds of times, I am able to smoothly connect the chair to the docking station.

Our first venture in the van was a trip to Gloria's house for Thanksgiving. This provided a few moments of stress. Loading into the van was no problem. The drive was not an issue. Sarah reported that the van drove normally, even though there was a lot of extra weight because of the ramps, hydraulics, etc. We pulled into the driveway and everyone gathered around to check out our new wheels and to greet us. Sarah opened the ramp door and the ramp lowered to the ground. It was then that we realized we had no idea how to get my wheelchair free from the docking station. My brother-in-law Rich is very handy around mechanical issues and even he was having difficulty. After what seemed like an eternal amount of pushing every button we saw, finally, a nondescript red button was discovered on the dashboard between the steering wheel and the driver's door. We also discovered that the driver's door had to be open for the button to work properly. Why no one explained this to us when the van was delivered is still a mystery. We were no doubt so excited about the whole van experience that we didn't hear that part of the instructions. After we all collectively exhaled with relief, I carefully backed out away from the docking station and made my way down the ramp to dinner.

We did, however, discover one potentially dangerous combination of my wheelchair's technology and entry to the van. When not used properly, the ability to raise the wheelchair up and down, as described earlier, can be quite dangerous. After eating dinner at a high-top table, I had raised the chair but forgot to lower it before heading up the ramp. I just about decapitated myself when I hit the top of the doorway with the middle of my face. Luckily, I was able to take my hand off the joystick and yell out to Sarah who was on the other side of the van. She backed me up and I lowered the chair. This is a lesson well learned and has stuck with me ever since. Now, I always verify that the wheelchair is at its lowest point before I head up the ramp.

*Celebrate what you have accomplished
but raise the bar a little higher
each time you succeed*

—Mia Hamm

CHAPTER 9
Christmas at MFB

Sarah keeps track of just about everything involving my care in a journal. Lots of information is exchanged in our day-to-day encounters and having a written log of things that were discussed proved invaluable. She tracks my future schedule, milestones I have completed, doctor's visits.... The list goes on and on. She continues to do that today. It has become especially helpful when dealing with insurance companies. They don't always remember what they promised. It is nice to keep track of the people we speak to and any commitments they may have made.

Christmas was approaching and I continued my six days-a-week of therapy. I continued breaking all of my individual records along the way (which Sarah was certain to keep track of in her journal). We had a night out with several patients attending a Grand Rapids Griffins minor-league hockey game. There was no stress attached to this outing as we took the MFB bus and were escorted by several therapists and techs. This was my first sporting event and it was difficult to tell if the experience was normal or was it radically different when traveling with several other patients and able-bodied therapists. I suspect that this experience was considerably different than doing it on my own.

Christmas was here and if patients were able, they were allowed to temporarily discharge to spend time at home with their families. I was perfectly happy to stay so that I could continue receiving therapy and have medical support if needed. We were able to use the Activities of Daily Living (ADL) room for a family Christmas gathering. The ADL room is where patients learn how to cook amongst many other day-to-day tasks. Just about everything you would need in a kitchen could be found there. Most importantly an oven. My parents, Alyson, Andy and Matthew spent the day with us. It was an unusual location for Christmas dinner but as with everything else we turned it into a positive and had a great day.

Two notable events occurred on December 30. My release date was extended for three more weeks. More exciting however, was my first time standing at a platform walker without the aid of a harness. A platform walker is the basic metallic walker that you have seen multiple senior citizens use, usually with tennis balls attached to the bottom. The platform walker differs due to extensions that raise up out of the walker base with troughs on top of the extensions for me to lay my forearms in. Although I could not grip, there were foam rubber handles for me to wrap my hands around. My arms were able to stay in the troughs due to leather straps wrapped around my arms and Velcroed in place securely.

My legs were supported by braces that looked like they were used in the Civil War. They were made of metal and plastic which were wrapped around my lower legs and feet with leather straps to secure them in place. The straps were stained from years of use. If this had been my first interaction at MFB I would have had some serious concerns about the poor condition of their equipment. Since there was no harness reducing my weight, this was the closest I have come to actually walking. This was a very difficult task and continues to be to this day. There was a lot going on simultaneously. I had to tuck my butt in and bring my shoulder blades back to stand tall. Sarah preferred to tell me to stick my boobies out rather than refer to my shoulder blades coming back. Standing tall makes it easier for me to swing my leg through. It was very easy for me to cheat and collapse on one side, but I paid for it when having to pull that leg through. Relearning to walk was difficult then and continues to be my most difficult task. Toddlers make it look awfully easy.

I continued the recovery progression and started walking with the help of a piece of equipment called the Tolos. The Tolos provides no weight support, but does include a harness should I make some type of mistake and start to fall. I used the walker with the Tolos for a short time until graduating to walking with only the platform walker and someone at each of my sides in case of emergency. Each time I progressed to the next walking support system I felt exhilarated and ready for the next challenge.

Once a month, the recreational therapist scheduled peer-to-peer meetings amongst any patients that were interested in attending. They were led by Caitlin, my recreational therapist. Dinner was always provided to help encourage patients and families to attend. These meetings were a great source of inspiration for me. The majority of patients in attendance also shared my optimism. Patients that hadn't quite accepted their situation usually left each meeting a little more positive after hearing others upbeat stories.

The hallways and therapy rooms of the third floor didn't cover too much area, so there were several interactions with my fellow patients on a daily basis. We had all seen each other in the various therapy rooms or in the hallways. There was one particular patient that got my attention. I referred to as "The Cowboy". This was due to the cowboy hat he always wore. He was a paraplegic and was very adept at moving his manual wheelchair through the halls. He was very cheerful and greeted everyone he saw. I overheard someone ask him how he could be so upbeat considering his condition. He replied, "I'm paralyzed. I can be miserable and paralyzed or I can be upbeat and paralyzed. I choose to be happy!" I've never forgotten The Cowboy or the positive examples he exhibited on a daily basis.

Another patient that made a lasting impact on me was a young man named Michael. Michael was in and out of the rehabilitation hospital. He was about 18 years old and had cerebral palsy from birth. Sometimes I saw him using his wheelchair and other times he was using walking braces and crutches. Michael went all over the hospital greeting other patients and talking with the medical staff. He had two catchphrases that could be heard throughout the third floor. He liked to say, "BOOM" and "Give it to me!" Sarah and I always enjoyed our interactions with Michael, he never ran out of stories to tell. I told him he was the "Mayor of MFB". The night before Michael was to be discharged, he stopped in to see me. After sharing our goodbyes, he said "Keith, now you are the Mayor of MFB." We both smiled widely.

One thing that became evident very early during my time at MFB was that no matter how bad my condition was, there were many others that were worse off. This was never more evident than in the case of a young man that had been in the rehab hospital for quite some time, but I did not see him very often. I finally heard his story through a third-party. He was a lineman for one of the utility companies. While working, he contacted a power line causing burns all over his body. To make matters worse, he was propelled out of the bucket truck he was working in and fell to the ground. That fall caused complete quadriplegia. To this day, if I ever start feeling sorry for myself, I think about what he must be going through.

The final patient's story that I would like to share involves a young woman in her 30s. She had been in a car accident but her injuries were quite minor compared to the rest of the people I saw each day. The treat she brought us was her toddler daughter. This sweet girl was very vocal and we were all aware when she was visiting her mom. That little girl brought a lot of smiles to a place where they were needed most. She got lots of visitors every time she stopped in. Sarah was usually leading the charge.

Seeing the other patients while we all worked in the gym was a great source of motivation for me. We may not have known each other by name but we all exchanged greetings and silently monitored each other's progress while comparing our injuries to others. There was a lot of encouragement between the patients. We were a little family that none of us had asked to join.

I was on several different medicines to help with muscle spasms and muscle tightness. If you ever see me have a spasm you may be scared. My hands tremble and shake violently and sometimes my entire body spasms. After a spasm, my body becomes extremely tight and it is difficult for me to move for several minutes. To help with these, I was told that my best option would be to use a surgically implanted baclofen pump. Baclofen was one of the oral medications I was already on. The pump would deliver the medication faster and in a higher concentration. Additionally, implanting the pump would mean one less pill that had to be metabolized through my liver.

The neurosurgeon explained the process. He showed me the actual device which was round and metallic. It resembled a hockey puck. The incision would be made in my abdomen at about the level of my bellybutton. It didn't matter which side of my abdomen was used but, in my case, it would be the left. The surgeon would create a "pocket" under my skin for the pump to rest. A catheter would lead from the pump to my spine where it would be threaded upwards along my spine as high as possible. The pump can be communicated with by using a special tablet-like device placed over the pump. It would take 7 to 10 days to manipulate the dosage of the baclofen until they found the optimum level. Every patient is different, so there is no regular dosage amount. One of the things that doctors worry about is going too far with the baclofen which would make my muscles too loose and would make it difficult for me to stand, walk and participate in therapy. Too loose? I wonder every day what that would feel like.

My surgery was set for February 1. It would be performed at Butterworth Hospital in Grand Rapids and would require an overnight stay. As an aside, the surgeon mentioned that the pump needed to be replaced every 5 to 6 years. I didn't like how he slid that information in, but what could I do? The reason for the replacement was battery life. The doctor told me that once a person has a baclofen pump it would be very, very rare for them not to need it for the rest of their life. This landed on me heavily. Just another reminder that my "condition" was never going away. I quickly switched gears to hopeful and realized that this would make my life much easier.

The surgery was successful and the catheter was placed at T1 on my spine. The postoperative experience was much more difficult. I spent seven days on my back due to spinal headaches. Due to the loss of therapy, my discharge date was moved back two weeks to February 18. Later, the date was moved back to March 3. There would be no more extensions after that.

The time for leaving our cocoon at Mary Free Bed was fast approaching and Sarah and I were scared to death. The bulk of the time at my remaining therapies was used to train Sarah on the various tasks she would have to undertake. It was a very hands-on experience for her. She had always been a voracious notetaker and she was in overdrive now. She was beginning to feel a little overwhelmed with all of the tasks she would now have to do. At MFB I had several people doing several different things, once we leave MFB it would only be Sarah and I.

One of the traditions for any patient leaving MFB was for the staff to paint the patient's toenails. I don't know how they decided who got what toe, but by the time they were finished I was a living piece of modern art. As a thank you, we bought lunch for everyone on one of my final days. It was more and more difficult each day realizing that I may never see this awesome group of people, my family, again.

I'd like to recognize each of the wonderful people that I worked with during my 6 ½ month stay at MFB. This could be a dangerous undertaking for two reasons. First, I will no doubt omit some of my team. I apologize for that upfront. Second, you, my dear reader, might not care one bit about a list of names. I don't blame you, but please indulge me. These amazing people were put on earth to make a difference in the lives of so many. I feel blessed that they were all part of my story.

Therapists: Ashley, Laura, Tracy, Tracey, Alice, Jamie, Christy, Mark, Jennifer, Shannon and Diane.

Nurses: Jessica, Jessica, Audra, Lisa, Leslie, Jenny, Christina, Catherine, Katharine, Sarah, Mel, Melissa, Cherie, Lisette, Lauren and Andrew.

Techs: Matthew, Troy, Rachel, Becca, Lyndon, Janae, Danielle, Danielle, Riley, Carrie, Brandon, Ashleigh, Catherine, Audrey, Mallory, Shae, Chrissy, Paige and Hannah.

As we work to create light for others, we naturally light our own Way

—M. Radmacher

A Portion of My Amazing Therapy Team

CHAPTER 10
Heading Home

It was March 3, 2016. Normally, the day a person gets released from the hospital would be a joyous occasion but I am not going to lie to you, Sarah and I were very nervous about what was to come. Now we had to do everything for ourselves. Where would Becca be to get me dressed? Who would bring me my dinosaur chicken nuggets? What time would Troy stop by to do my bowel program? The answer to all of these was "sorry kid you are on your own now". Sarah pulled the van around to the front of the hospital. With help, she made several trips to take all of my belongings for loading in the van. It was surprising how much stuff we had accumulated during our stay. Sarah always kept the room nicely decorated. The room always looked homey, very un-hospital looking. Many people commented how inviting my room always looked. To encourage visitors, Sarah always kept a bowl full of candy for others to enjoy. The staff would often stop by for a quick "pick me up".

We couldn't put it off any longer. Sarah transferred me into my wheelchair and we headed down the hallway. We spent so much time in room 3138 that we have expected it to be renamed the Stone Strong suite.

The staff lined up on each side cheering us on and giving us high-fives. Or at least as high as I could do them. Arriving at the van, thankfully our audience had dwindled. Having fewer witnesses to one of my early attempts to drive up the ramp and dock in the van was a good thing as far as I was concerned. It took me three or four attempts until I heard the "click" of the wheelchair post successfully connecting. Sarah started up the van and we began the 2 ½ hour trip to Grand Blanc. It was a quiet ride home. At one point Sarah looked at me and said, "How could they be sending us home? Why are they trusting me to take care of you?" We were very emotional and quite nervous about leaving the safety of our cocoon at Mary Free Bed. But we knew we would get through by trusting in ourselves and even more importantly trusting in the Lord.

Throughout the winter my parents braved the cold weather of Michigan to supervise the changes made to our brand-new condo back in Grand Blanc in order to make it more accessible for me. There were numerous changes that had to be made and it was comforting to have two supervisors on site to oversee the work. Those changes included a ramp in the garage leading into the house, wider doorways, special hinges on the doors that allow them to open much wider. The doors had a "zero threshold" so that there was no bump whatsoever when going through a door. The door to the garage had a power arm attached to it so that I could open it with the touch of a button. I had to have a second exit in case of a fire. So, there was another ramp from the house to the rear patio. A 115' long sidewalk was installed from the rear patio wrapping around the house to the driveway. This was also to help facilitate my ability to exit in case of a fire or some other emergency.

There was no carpeting in the house whatsoever. Earlier, after taking possession of the condo, Sarah enlisted Carmela and her husband Michael to rip out the flooring of the two rooms that did have carpeting. Sarah had coordinated with Home Depot so that they would install hardwood floor just two days after the carpeting had been pulled up. It was much easier for me to get the wheelchair around the house on tile or hardwood floors. This would also be easier for me when I started to use a walker to get around. A permanent ceiling track lift was installed above my bed. It was exactly like the one I had at Mary Free Bed. This was used to get me out of bed via a sling for showers or any emergencies in which I couldn't transfer to my wheelchair with my normal squat pivot.

A squat pivot consists of putting a gait belt around my waist. Sarah did most of the heavy lifting but my legs were a bit helpful. To get into bed Sarah and I worked to get me to the edge of the wheelchair seat. She grabbed the belt by putting her arms around me and on a count of three I would stand and she would immediately turn me towards the bed and put me down. It took some additional manipulation to get me into the spot in the bed.

To get me back into the chair the gait belt was used once again. The most difficult part of this process was getting me from a laying position up to sitting on the edge of the bed. My core muscles were weak and most of the burden was on Sarah. Once I was on the edge of the bed, I would stand and Sarah would turn me and put me down in the chair. There was rarely a perfect landing so we would have to tilt the chair and Sarah would pull me into the proper position. Once I was properly placed into the chair, I drove to the family room and tilted back as far as possible letting my arms hang down over the armrests to stretch my pectoral muscles. This is still our process to this day.

The existing traditional swinging door to the bathroom was replaced with a barn style sliding door mounted on a rail above the door. This gave me plenty of room to get through the doorway whether in a shower chair or a wheelchair. The shower was a zero-threshold roll-in shower. This meant that there was no lip whatsoever between the shower floor and the bathroom floor. You may have seen step in showers advertised on television but they have a very slight barrier to keep the water in the tub. This was nothing like that. My shower chair could be rolled directly into the shower. This was one of the most attractive features that Sarah came across when she was looking for our next home. With no lip, taking a bath was out of the question. Only showers. That was fine for me. I'm not a big fan of sitting in my own filth.

Sarah had been in constant communication with the medical equipment company that would be delivering all of the equipment I needed when I went home. Every time my length of stay was extended, Sarah would let the company know. Coordination with the medical equipment supplier was perfectly executed and by the time Sarah and I had arrived it had all been delivered. This included my shower chair, my manual wheelchair, a hospital bed and a portable Hoyer lift.

The hospital bed has all the functions of a normal hospital bed. There were manually operated rails on each side of the bed. All of the other functions were activated via electronic motors. My head and feet could be raised or lowered, the entire bed could be raised or lowered. The raising and lowering of the bed was important for getting me in and out of bed and also Sarah needed the bed in a higher position when moving me around to ease the stress on her back.

The Hoyer lift could be moved around the house and used for the same functions as the built-in overhead lift in the bedroom. We had used one at MFB but we wondered when we would ever use this and we felt it was a waste of the insurance company's money. Little did we know at the time.

Later in the afternoon, after going over every piece of new equipment and touring our new home, we decided to settle in and watch television. Sarah had bought me a very comfortable looking chair. This chair had a remote control to manipulate its many functions. One of these functions is to raise and lower the seat to help a person get in and out of the chair.

Sounds perfect for me! We mentally rehearsed my transfer to the chair and began. Shortly into the process things went horribly wrong. Sarah and my dad couldn't hold me up and my legs weren't strong enough to do it on their own. We were in trouble. It was a nice slow-motion fall as Sarah and my dad were able to slowly guide me down to the floor. So rather than sitting in the nice fluffy chair I ended up on the floor. What a great time to have a Hoyer portable lift!

After the laughter subsided, Sarah began the process of getting me into the sling that we were certain we wouldn't need. Sarah rolled me back and forth on the floor to get me into the sling. One of Sarah's trainings at MFB was how to load me into a sling. She knew what she was doing. There were four hooks on the sling. The sling had to be placed behind my back. I had to lean forward as far as possible so Sarah could get the sling behind me. Two of the hooks on the sling were for my upper body and two were for my legs. It was very important that the two straps for my legs were crossed over each other. Otherwise, I would have fallen right out of the sling.

Once I was set up in the sling, we attempted to put me back in the lazy boy chair. There was a remote on the lift to raise me high enough to put me in the chair that. However, the legs on the chair and the legs on the lift didn't line up properly. We aborted that attempt and I was lowered back into my wheelchair.

I don't exactly remember what made us think we could pull off this transfer the second time but we gave it our best shot. Just as the previous attempt, I ended up on the floor and the "unnecessary" lift rescued me for a second time. To this day, I have rarely sat in that chair. Guests seem to enjoy it however.

Sarah seemed to know just about everyone in Grand Blanc. To our delight, one of them set up a meal train. A meal train is simply a list of people signing up to bring a meal to someone. In this case we were the lucky recipients. The list was long and the food selections varied. I don't think we cooked a meal for three months. No matter what we tried to think of to thank all these great people, none were interested in anytime of reciprocation. They were all happy to do it and we felt very blessed to have such a great support group. Yet another example of the Gospel according to Sarah; making connections with people was important!

One of the biggest changes to my personality since the accident was a greater sense of empathy. Sarah had always handled that in amounts so great that I didn't need to participate. Seeing all the support and love from friends, family and medical professionals really hit home for me. I suppose it was about time. I was turning into my wife. I could do a lot worse than that. I knew I was a complete convert when we were watching a sad movie and I began crying. I had never done that before. All I could say was, "Empathy sucks!" Sarah comforted me with a hug.

I no longer had Dr. Ho at my beck and call for medical services. I needed to find a physiatrist closer to home. We asked Dr. Ho for some help in locating one on our side of the state. He recommended Dr. Jennifer Doble. She had visited his clinic in the past so he had some personal knowledge of her. However, the pickings were slim and there were not a lot to choose from according to Dr. Ho. Dr. Doble worked in Ann Arbor about one hour from our home. A physiatrist is essential to my care. They know more than any other doctor about spinal cord injuries and a physiatrist monitors my baclofen pump and refills it as necessary. This needed to be done every two months or so. It was a very simple process but required some complex equipment.

To refill the pump the doctor placed a piece of equipment on my abdomen over the location of the pump. It looked like a piece of plastic connected to an iPad. My pump is located on my front left side about bellybutton high. The pump has a small covered opening in which the doctor semi-blindly inserts a small needle to remove the baclofen currently in my pump. She measures this to ensure that the pump is delivering the medicine at the correct rate. Delivering more or less than expected indicates a problem. Assuming this checks out, she inserts another needle into the pump to deliver fresh baclofen ready for use. It is important that I stay vigilant in keeping the pump filled with medicine as withdrawals from a lack of the medication can be life-threatening. Dr. Doble cautioned us that the three signs of a withdrawal are itchy, bitchy and twitchy. She implored us to get medical attention if I felt these.

Just because I was home, it did not mean that my days of therapy were over. Now I began the journey of outpatient therapy. More difficult than the therapy was the constant communication with the insurance company to continue to provide the therapy I needed. Initially, the approvals for outpatient therapy from the insurance company were easy. Obviously, a person just released from over six months in an inpatient setting would need continued rehab. I had gone from six hours a day of therapy to 4 to 6 hours per week. I was not happy about this but it started to show us how heavy the burden was going to land on Sarah and I to do more things at home.

You may never notice a therapy facility as you drive down the road, but there are plenty of them out there. After some consultation with friends, reviews on the internet and visitations we selected STAR; Strength Training and Rehabilitation. STAR was located nearby and was in the same building as the health club I had attended prior to my accident. Insurance had approved three one-hour sessions per week.

STAR had a lot of the same equipment I used at MFB. We spent the majority of our time continuing walking with the platform walker and strengthening my body. Sophia was the very flamboyant owner and all of the therapists and assistant therapists (OTA) seemed to get my humor. Sophia had quite a collection of footwear and it was always interesting to see what she had on from one day to the next. I soon became very comfortable with our workout routine. I did most of my work there with Erin, Adam and Lewis.

Unfortunately, there were plenty of setbacks during that first-year home. On April 20, Sarah noticed a sore on the bottom of my right foot directly below my little toe. Doctors tried healing it with a variety of remedies including collagen. None of them were effective and I was grounded. That first pressure sore kept me off my feet for eight weeks. The sore reappeared in mid-August, preventing me from walking for an additional four weeks. This is still a reoccurring nuisance in my recovery and we have to keep a very close eye on their development.

Also, during this time, I had quite a bit of tightness in my chest specifically my pectorals. It made it difficult for me to use my arms. Dr. Doble recommended I try a Botox injection. I've always wanted to look younger, so I very eagerly agreed. I was quickly brought back to earth when the doctor explained to me this type of injection was intended to loosen the muscles in my chest. We tried this procedure several times with only short-term positive results. I still get Botox injections to this day. They do seem to help but they aren't a miracle cure. Sarah gets Botox injections for her migraine headaches. Who knew Botox could do so much?

November, 2016 brought more challenging times. All of the tightness I had experienced in my muscles I was now experiencing in my diaphragm. The diaphragm is the muscle group we all use to breathe. That is where you got hit if you ever had the wind knocked out of you. My diaphragm was so tight that it was all I could do to grab even the tiniest breath. Sarah called 911 and calmly walked me through some breathing techniques. We had learned these somewhere along the line and I was grateful that she was able to recall them. The technique involved breathing in and out through my mouth while forming an "O" with my mouth. I was so focused on her that I didn't realize the EMTs had arrived. I was feeling much better by this point. They took my vitals, which had returned to normal by now and confirmed that I did not want to be taken to the hospital. That was the closest I had felt to death since the day of my accident. I asked Sarah how she could remain so calm, and without hesitation she told me we weren't alone during that incident. She felt God's presence.

Two weeks later, I experienced the same feeling. However, this time I was still in distress when the ambulance arrived. A trip to the hospital was necessary this time. Eventually, my vitals again returned to normal and I was released the next day. Breathing techniques, Sarah and God had guided me through another crisis.

I couldn't continue going through these episodes. Dr. Doble finally found the problem after several weeks of tests. It wasn't until December 28, more than four weeks since my last breathing episode, that a cause was found. A CT scan revealed a problem with the catheter leading from my baclofen pump. There was a crack in the catheter and the medicine was not being delivered as intended. Remember those life-threatening withdrawals I referred to earlier?

On January 12, 2017 I underwent surgery at St. Joseph's Hospital in Ann Arbor. The catheter replacement surgery was simple and successful. I have not had an issue with it since. While the surgery was simple, the recovery was much more difficult. It was quite an undertaking to titrate my pump to release the correct amount of baclofen. After one week, I had planned to go home but I was still suffering very painful headaches while the correct dosage of the medicine was determined. My doctor thought it would be best for me to stay an additional week. She reasoned that while I was in the hospital medical personnel would be able to more aggressively adjust my level of baclofen since I was being monitored so closely. Going home would make the adjustments a much slower process. Sarah stayed with me, once again sleeping in my room for the entire duration of my stay.

I had 2 to 4 hours of therapy each day during my second week at St. Josephs. I had a chance to work with another great therapist. Her name was Lindsay and she was a hockey player. She had no difficulty throwing me around during our bedside sessions. We never left the room for therapy. I finally went home January 27.

We spend the rest of the winter months with my parents in Florida. I continued outpatient physical therapy while there. Rather than muddy the waters by involving a facility in a different state we decided to pay them directly. We were not especially impressed. However, just getting out of the house and stretching was beneficial.

The warm weather and wide, quiet streets enabled me to do some therapy on my own. My manual wheelchair can be set up with normal wheels like you have seen thousands of times before. I do not have the strength to push the wheels on that type of chair. However, I have a secret weapon. I also have a pair of "E-motion" wheels. These wheels are motorized and enhance the pushes that I provide. With a good push I can move about 10 feet. I eventually built up my stamina and went around my parents block which was about .4 miles in length.

When we returned home from Florida, Sarah and I decided to make a change in our outpatient PT provider. After two years, I felt like my therapy at STAR was growing stale. I appreciate everything they did for me at STAR. We started to look for something new. It was time for some fresh ideas. Amazingly, there was another facility in Grand Blanc that dealt with neurological patients. After a tour revealed impressive equipment and a young, enthusiastic staff, we decided to make the move to Level 11 in early 2018. I never asked, but I hope their name was a reference to the movie "Spinal Tap". If you are unfamiliar with that cinematic classic, the bands guitar amps volume went all the way up to 11. "Because, you know it's one more than 10." Brilliant! My sarcasm should fit right in.

Therapists must either take on the personalities of their clients or they are all just a bunch of sarcastic goofballs like myself. At Level 11 I worked with Mandy and her PTA Randi. They could almost pass for sisters. I worked with a lot of therapists that were fun to be around to this point, but these two took the cake. However, when it came to my therapy, they certainly knew their stuff. Mandy was big into horses and I enjoyed hearing her stories. Randi was just plain fun and her laugh would echo throughout the gym. STAR was fantastic for me but the decision to make the change was the correct one. It is beneficial to get a new perspective from time to time. We still keep in touch with each other through Facebook. There was also a PTA that I worked with, Luis, whom I still stay in touch with.

All of these challenges on the road to a smooth recovery may have knocked me back, but they never knocked me out. I knew that combining hard work the help of the medical profession, Sarah and God, that things would improve for me. Some days it is harder for me to believe that than others but I never lose faith. I never lose hope. I always stayed optimistic.

*Struggles not only make us into stronger,
better and wiser people,
they also let us learn more about
ourselves and
our purpose in life*

—Auliq Ice

CHAPTER 11
Super Sarah

I have been doing a lot of talking about the things I go through each day but let's talk about the real hero, Sarah. While there is certainly no predictable, typical day for Sarah and I, here is a look at some of the things she does for me on a daily basis. Almost everyone's wedding vows include a part about loving each other in both sickness and health. Sarah never wavered from those vows.

Everything she does for me is above and beyond the normal household duties that any couple would share. Things like cooking, shopping, cleaning, laundry and a million other little things too numerous to list. I considered myself to be helpful around the house and tried to contribute in any way that I could. Now she handles 100% of these tasks. The worst nights are garbage nights. It was always my job to empty all the cans in the house and then transport the large collection bin down to the curb. At least four months of the year this has to be done in freezing weather. After coming inside on those very cold night I would exclaim, "It's a good night not to be homeless". These are my saddest times. I sit in a cozy room watching TV while she has to run out into the cold.

Another mundane task is the laundry. I used to work from home on Fridays and I would do all the laundry by the time Sarah got home. Now that all falls on to Sarah. It seems like there is at least one load to do each day.

Every night we look at our first appointment of the following day and set the alarm for three hours prior to that. Sarah likes to get up an hour before I do so she can eat breakfast and just have some calm time to herself. She often reads devotionals during that time. On a good day, it takes 30 minutes to get me out of bed and ready for the day. I like to have 30 to 60 minutes before we head out the door.

We sometimes watch the ID channel while getting ready in the morning but we usually listen to music with the help of our Alexa device. Sarah's favorites are Tim McGraw or Ed Sheeran. I like Motown and I also have a playlist of several dozen of my favorite songs. "Thunderstruck" by AC/DC and "What I Like About You" by The Romantics are excellent up-tempo songs that help to get me going.

The first task each morning usually involves my eyes. Every morning they are difficult to open and they burn. Sarah is very aware of this as I stare at her with one eye tightly shut. I ask Sarah to do things that she already knows needs to be done but I do it anyways. A lot of times when this happens, she will tell me "This isn't my first rodeo". It's quite a challenge to bite my tongue knowing that Sarah will eventually complete each task on her mental checklist. I often fail at this.

Next, she empties urine from my large night bag into the toilet. Often times she uses the restroom herself (selfish!). The toilet is about 20 feet from my head so she doesn't get much privacy. I try not to stare. Before attaching the urine bag that I wear during the day to my catheter she sterilizes the tip of my Foley bag with an alcohol wipe. This is an important part of the process to prevent those nasty UTIs. She reattaches the bag to my leg with two Velcro straps.

I drink about a liter of Gatorade each night. Sarah came up with a way for me to drink fluids both in bed during the night and in my wheelchair during the day. A plastic container is hooked to the side of my bed and a hose with a nozzle is attached to my arm so I can easily get a drink. The container is set aside before we can continue.

Sarah removes the four braces from my hands and feet. The foot braces keep my ankles bent to prevent foot drop. They are made of parachute like material and secured with Velcro. The hand braces keep my wrists slightly bent and prevent my fingers from balling up into a fist. The braces are very heavy but they keep my hands in place. Every morning when she takes them off my hands spasm and tighten up. Occasionally, my head itches and I scratch so hard during the night that the Velcro eventually surrenders leaving my hand turned completely around in the brace. I try to play it off and in my best Urkel voice I say, "did I do that?"

If one of the hand braces falls off, the dominoes of doom continue to fall when I realize that I can now bite my fingernails. This has been a bad habit of mine for my entire life. On one occasion I got a stern talking to from my primary care physician because I had chewed into my skin and caused an infection to develop. Sarah reminds me of this often. When I was a kid, my mom always threatened to put red pepper on my fingertips but she never followed through. I love you mom!

The next step in our morning routine is taking my pills. I have quite a morning cocktail of medicine. I take these pills with a protein drink. The chocolate drinks are quite delicious and loaded with protein. Through trial and error, Sarah helped me learn how to swallow numerous pills at once. Here is the morning roster. First, the prescription drugs:

- Pepcid (Famotidine) -Prevent acid reflux
- Lipitor (Atorvastatin)-Cholesterol
- Eliquis (Apixaban)-to prevent blood clots

- Keppra (Levetiracetam)-for TGA's or memory issues
- Restasis (Cyclosporine) Eye drops
- Buspar (Buspirone)-Anti-depression
- Prilosec (Omeprozale)-Digestion

Over-the-counter drugs

- Cranberry pills-UTI's
- D-Mannose-UTI's
- Fibercon-Bowels
- Flonase-Nasal spray
- Probiotic-Digestion
- Zyrtec-Allergies
- Airborne gummies-Probiotic
- Vitamin D-Bone density
- Magnesium

Whew! Now, Sarah dresses me. Don't get too excited but at night I sleep naked from the waist down! I have already put on today's shirt the previous night because it is easier to do sitting up in the wheelchair as opposed to laying down in the bed. Socks are first item to be put on but not just normal easy to put on socks. No, I must have compression socks. Compression socks help with blood flow but are much more difficult to put on simply because they are so tight and they go all the way up to my knees. Then boxers and almost always sweatpants. I rarely wear shorts because of my Foley bag. I hate to look at it and I can only imagine someone else having to look at. I do have underwear that would allow me to tuck the bag away but I have had problems with kinking of the tube when using that.

I made that sound like an easy routine but of course it isn't. Getting my pants on is the most difficult of those tasks. Sarah has to move from one side of the bed to the other turning me on my side and alternately pulling up my pants inch by inch. I try to help by reaching my hand over the rail and holding myself up. Some days are better than others. Until recently, I wore XXL shirts because they are easier to get on and off (plus I eat a lot of ice cream).

I used to be able to shave myself using an electric shaver attached to my hand by a cloth band that wraps around the shaver with the help of Velcro. This is called a Palmer band. However, I can't reach some of the spots on my face any longer so Sarah had started shaving me in bed. No electric shaver can manage the clean look of a shave with a blade. Very recently, based on a recommendation from Andy, Sarah started shaving me the old-fashioned way with shaving cream and "Harry's" razors. She does this for me three or four times a week. Replacement blades are automatically sent to our home periodically.

After lying in bed for 8 to 10 hours my body becomes tight. The rolling back and forth sends me into mild spasms and makes me incredibly tight. To help loosen me for the transfer to the wheelchair, Sarah grabs my feet and pumps my legs at the knee. She also stretches my fingers and wrists. Next, she puts on my shoes and attaches the gait belt around my waist. Then we do the squat pivot that I described earlier. Morning transfers are much more difficult than when I go to bed. We have had some close calls over the years but we have never failed to get me into the wheelchair. There are days when my right leg refuses to cooperate. On those days, it can be very difficult for Sarah to lift my foot up onto the footplate of the chair. My best efforts to help with that movement often times fail. My left leg is looser and that side is much easier for her to manipulate. Now I have safely transferred into the wheelchair but I am by no means ready to go. The squat pivot leaves me in a slouched position. Sarah adjusts the wheelchair so that I am sitting almost horizontally to the floor. This takes gravity out of the equation. We do one or two more coordinated lifts and leg pushes until I am sitting up straight and we can successfully buckle the seatbelt. I drive the chair out of the bedroom to the television and get caught up on the previous days sporting events with ESPN.

At last, one might think Sarah has some time to relax! Not so fast my friend. Now she has to get herself ready for the day plus make our beds and put my dirty clothes in the hamper.

When Sarah comes out, she has my electric toothbrush ready to go. I am able to hold it with the use of a Palmer band similar to the one that I described earlier when using my razor. This band has a slot for the toothbrush. She puts the toothpaste on the bristle and I am able to move it around and get most of my not so pearly whites cleaned up. I rinse with water and Listerine.

Now it is caffeine time! A large cup of coffee makes me feel ready for the day. At this time, I eat my second breakfast (I consider the protein drink my first breakfast). Usually something sweet like a cinnamon crumb cake, pop tart or mini muffins. Each day is different at this point. I usually don't like leaving the house but when I do it always seems to loosen me up. The gentle vibrations of riding in the van help with that. The not so gentle vibrations however, send me into arm spasms. A rough railroad track, pothole, or God forbid, a speedbump are all very rough on me. Through time I have learned that the effect is lessened if I lift my arms up off of the wheelchair and just let them float through the turbulence.

Our schedule is different each day but believe it or not, there are days when Sarah (deservedly) takes a mental health break and will go out on her own and do whatever she pleases. She worries about me when she does this, but it really isn't an issue. I am unable to use a traditional remote control for the TV. I use Alexa to help me navigate through the television channels with verbal commands. Matthew bought a camera so that Sarah can check up on me if she is ever out of the house for an extended period of time. She feels better running out knowing that she can always check on me. She can even talk to me through the Alexa devices.

I am so thankful for the technology of an Apple iPhone and iPad. It is very easy for me to type using the keyboard or using the vocal commands. I am able to read and respond to emails. I am able to easily navigate through Facebook. I try to post witty comments and I think they work because no one has unfriended me yet. I also play Sudoko, Wordle, chess or a game called Immaculate Grid. It revolves around athletes. I usually play the baseball version. Basically, there is a grid of nine squares that you have to fill in the proper player for each intersection. For example, a player that has played at least one game for the Tigers and at least one game for the Yankees. Others involve statistics such as a team's 20 game winners or 30 stolen bases. I have played it around 50 times and only got an immaculate grid twice.

Sarah probably winces a little every time she comes home because I always have a lengthy list of tasks that I need her to do for me. "Sarah, I need some more drink. Sarah, my Foley bag needs emptied. Sarah, the tube on my drink has slid out of the holder. Sarah, what kind of chocolate do we have?" The list goes on and on. One thing that seems to happen every time is that after I give her that long list and she thinks she's done I say "one more thing". She is used to it now but it doesn't make her any happier.

Communicating my needs is a tight-rope walk. Sarah is a self-proclaimed "now girl". She assumes that any request I make needs to happen immediately. I have been trying to do better about that and I ask her, "The next time you are up please do X, Y and Z". Often times, this also leads to one more thing.

I skip lunch more often than not but I have been trying to do better. I never need a full meal but I do eat a Clif bar. They look horrible but they are chock-full of nutrients and protein. Oatmeal or peanut butter flavors are the best). We also both eat Built bars which are chocolatey and full of protein.

Sarah tends to make bulk meals for dinner. By that, I mean something we can eat for several nights in a row. Popular choices include: macaroni and cheese, taco salads, turkey roasts, beef roasts and ham. Grocery stores are a great source for ready-to-eat meals that only require heating in the oven. Occasionally, we buy junk out of the frozen food aisle such as potato skins, mozzarella sticks and pizza rolls. We snack on those and consider it a meal.

As far as fast food is considered, I enjoy Arby's beef and cheddar sandwich with curly fries. Nuggets from Chick-fil-A with waffle fries are also tasty. Regarding take-out from restaurants, my absolute go-to is a sandwich from Mancino's. The pizza sub is my favorite. I can get two meals out of one order. Day two would be just as tasty. Sarah always ordered a ham and cheese sub with lettuce only. She has done this for as long as I've known her.

The rest of the evening is spent playing on our phones and watching television. All of you people with androids are a pain in my butt! I always have to have my phone around because my preferred iPad cannot communicate with your stupid phone. I am talking to you Gil and Paul! Those two Griswold's split Detroit Lions season tickets. Along with Dave Smith, the four of us keep a running commentary going during the Lions game. Gil can find a meme or a GIF faster than anyone on the planet.

Sorry for the segue. Back to Sarah and I and our evening routine. Jeopardy is a must watch for us at 7:00. She usually goes to bed after Jeopardy for some more decompression time. I stay up for various amounts of time after she goes to bed. Football games get my attention. I also stream plenty of shows on Netflix, Hulu or Amazon prime. Commercial free programming is so nice.

Spending 24 hours per day together has caused some of my personality quirks to be picked up by Sarah. My favorite one is that she now has become quite adept at quoting TV shows and movies. I never thought she was listening when I did those day after day. Now she fires off a "don't call me Shirley" or one of the hundreds of Seinfeld lines I use on a daily basis. She makes me so proud! I could never love her any more than I do during those moments. However, she has strictly forbidden me from using Michael Scott's line used in The Office. There are so many times I want to say to her, "that's what she said". It's hard (that's what she said) but I have become adept at only using my inner voice in those situations.

Now it's time for me to go to bed. It's a 50/50 shot that she will be awake. I hate to wake her up but that doesn't stop me from doing it. The nighttime routine is quicker and easier than the morning. Sarah meets me at the bedroom door after I roust her from her slumber. She puts my devices on the chargers, grabs my laptop task and takes my reading glasses off. I drive the wheelchair as close as possible to the side of the bed. Sarah is boxed in by the bed, wheelchair and two walls. She removes the shirt I wore during the day. Some days this is more difficult than others depending on how tight my arms and chest are. She swipes deodorant under each arm pit (you're welcome). She puts my shirt on for the next day because as I mentioned it is easier to do that when my trunk is in an upright position rather than laying down. She grabs the gait belt and attaches it to my chest. Now we do the squat pivot into bed. This is much easier because we are going downhill and I am much looser. I lay down on my side, Sarah drives the wheelchair away from the bed and she grabs my feet and swings me over so that I am lying in bed on my back. I have slept on my back every day since my accident. Prior to that I had never slept on my back. She takes my pants and socks off which is considerably easier than putting them on.

By far, the most difficult part of our routine is my bowel program. I wouldn't blame you if you wanted to avoid reading about this part of our journey. Heck, I hate writing about it but it is what it is so here you go.(What follows was our routine before I had a procedure called a colostomy. You will hear more about that later).

If I haven't accidentally gone in my pants during the day I try to go at bedtime. Sarah rolls me onto my right side (through trial and error we have determined that the right side is better than the left). I lay there for a few minutes waiting to see if I can go. If that doesn't happen, the next step is to insert a suppository just as they did at MFB. Those bullets work pretty fast and if we time it right Sarah places a bedpan beneath me and she dumps it in the toilet and we are done for the next 24 to 48 hours. Ah, but that would be too easy. More often than not I have a bowel movement sometime later with very little warning. There is no bedpan in place, just an extra towel or sheet. A firm (so many words to choose from here) turd is much easier to deal with than looser stool or God forbid, diarrhea. Still with me? Good, moving on...

Some of my evening medicines are the same as the morning but there are a few differences. My evening medicine is taken with a mixture of cranberry juice, and Metamucil. Here is the rest of the list:

Prescription Drugs

- Valium (Diazepam)-for spasticity
- Pepcid
- Baclofen (Lioresal) this is a backup dosage in case my pump failed
- Ditropan (Oxybutyin)-for spastic bladder
- Lexapro (Escitalopram)-for anxiety
- Eliquis
- Keppra
- Restasis
- Remeron (Mirtazapine)-depression and promotes appetite.
- Omeprazole
- Buspirone

Over-the-counter

- Mannose
- Flonase

Just a quick word about mirtazapine. I've only taken it for a few months to help reengage my appetite. It has worked wonders in that department but one of the side effects that I have experienced have been horrible nightmares/dreams. I don't know if it is a known side effect but I do know what has happened to me. Probably five times a week, I wake up in a panic about something that happened during my sleep. Anything from a big project at work that I have completed to finding out one of my closest friends was a Nazi! I found this out by attending one of his family member's wedding. I am so relieved when I wake up and realize it was all just a dream. Now that my appetite has returned, I'm working to get off that drug.

When I was in college, Tuesday nights were Stromboli nights at Little Caesars pizza. They must have contained some of the same chemicals as mirtazapine because every Wednesday morning my roommate and I would wake up exchanging the details of our weird dreams.

Have you ever wondered why drugs have two names? One is a generic name that is limited by various prefixes and suffixes. The second name is a brand name. Pharmaceutical companies spend millions of dollars and several years to come up with the perfect brand name for their newest creation. For example, sildenafil is the generic name for Viagra. I spent several hours in that wormhole and while it was entertaining, I soon realized it was too complex to include in this book. I will leave any further research to you. One night when you are tired of the political yapping on Facebook look it up.

Next, Sarah puts a pillow under one of my hips to help prevent bedsores. Then she puts on the braces for my hands and feet. I usually fall asleep quite quickly. For whatever reason, I often wake up sometime between 3 AM and 4 AM. I often use the time to think of my next book. We have a digital clock in our room within my sightline but because my eyes are so crusty it is often difficult for me to read it. Apparently, Sarah was tired of hearing me ask Alexa what time it was during the middle of the night. She ordered a new clock with bright red numbers the size of an NBA shot clock. She was mocking me but I don't have to disturb her anymore. It is harder for me to sleep at this time and I am often left staring at the ceiling. It gives me some peace to hear Sarah fall asleep. Lord knows she deserves it.

A few times a week, depending on how early our daily appointments are scheduled to begin, Sarah gives me a shower. This adds about 60 minutes to our morning routine. We use a mesh sling powered by the lift over my bed to transfer me into a specialty shower chair. Getting into the sling requires the same multiple rolls back and forth similar to getting my pants on. The sling is mesh so that it dries quicker. The shower chair tilts back to make it easier to load me. This is not the plastic shower chair that we used at MFB. This one should have a Cadillac logo on it. It is made of stainless steel and the seat and arm rests are made of comfortable black faux leather. There are foot rests and arm rests. The cushioned seat has a hole cut in the middle with a plastic bowl below it should I decide to have a bowel movement in the shower. Just another glamorous part of our day. Sarah disconnects the sling from the lift, tips the chair up and rolls me into the shower. This is why a shower entrance that is even with the bathroom floor is so important. There is no way to get that chair into a shower with even the tiniest lip in the way.

The shower is equipped with a handheld shower head. Sarah sprays me along with several washcloths and a glove made out of washcloth material that I use to wash my chest, neck and arms. She then washes my hair. This is one of the favorite parts of my life! It feels so good when she gets the right spot. I must sound like Meg Ryan from the movie "When Harry Met Sally". You know the scene, don't pretend you don't know what I'm talking about.

Then she squirts body wash on my chest. While she gets my bed ready for my return, I attempt to wash my upper body. I call out when I am done with one side and she returns to the shower to put the glove on my other hand. Once Sarah is done preparing the bed, she washes my hair and cleans the areas I can't reach. Then she covers me in towels and we head back to the bed. She uses the trick we learned at MFB, laying the very large towels on the bed. Sarah hooks the lift back up to the mesh sling and lowers me back onto the bed. She dries off the front of my body while the towels I am laying on absorb the water from the back side of my body. A quick roll on each side to pull out the blankets and voilà we are able to begin our morning routine.

Every 3 to 4 weeks the silicone tube from my SP in my bladder to the Foley bag has to be replaced. She does this earlier if I have cloudy urine. Sarah learned how to do this while we were still at MFB and she is quite comfortable with the process. She uses a syringe to pull the water out of the small balloon that is holding my tube in place within my bladder. She expects to get 10 cc of fluid out of the balloon. If she pulls out something in that neighborhood, it is safe to remove the tube from my bladder. Only one time, very early in our experiences, did she try to pull out the balloon before it was empty. It was a surprising and slightly painful experience for me. However, it only happened that one time.

Once the old tube is removed, she coats the new tube with petroleum jelly and inserts it through the hole. My body definitely feels this and reacts with not-so-subtle spasms. Finally, she refills the balloon with 10 cc of sterile water. Sarah works very diligently to do all this while maintaining a sterile environment. The catheter goes directly into my bladder so we know how important keeping the tube clean and sterile is. The Foley bag is attached to my leg with two Velcro straps to complete the process.

We have different gifts according to the grace given to each of us

–Romans 12:6

CHAPTER 12

Wedding Day

The day that Sarah and I had looked forward to for so long had finally arrived. It was June 23, 2018. This was the day our son, Andrew, was marrying his beautiful bride, Alyson. This was the day all of my hard work would be put on display. It had been just over two years since their engagement. On that day I made a vow to dance at their wedding. Accomplishing that goal was my motivation during every PT session I had.

The day started cloudy with very light rainfall. This made everyone a bit nervous as the wedding ceremony was scheduled to take place outdoors, on the shore of picturesque Lake Walden. Weather conditions improved throughout the day and all in attendance were able to enjoy the afternoon event without any concerns. Sarah had put her parents, Harry and Marge, and our nephew Adam in charge of weather and they really came through for us as they looked down at the gathering from heaven.

I was very thankful that I felt great that entire weekend. The ceremony was perfect. Afterwards, we moved inside for the reception. I started getting a little nervous during dinner. Traditionally, the first dance is reserved for the bride and groom. This was no exception. This was followed by the bride's dance with her father, Kelly. Next was Sarah's dance with Andy. The two of them had taken a couple of lessons and learned their routine perfectly. I was proud of them but also unsure as to how I would live up to their performance. Most of the people there did not know that I was going to attempt to dance. So, it was a bit of a surprise when the DJ announced that Sarah and I would be dancing next. Everybody gathered around the dance floor. It was my moment of truth. Sarah and I had practiced this multiple times and she had complete confidence in me. I was wearing my gait belt underneath my suit coat. She grabbed it, we counted to three and I was on my feet. I was able to get my arms up onto her shoulders. There was a lot of emotion from the wedding guests. We danced to the same song we danced to over 30 years previously at our wedding. "Always and Forever" by Heat Wave. We had forgotten how long that song is. (Since that day I discovered that song is over six minutes long) I was running on fumes and people were probably getting tired of seeing us rocking back and forth. Andy and Alyson started dancing next to us until the conclusion of the song. This was one of my most triumphant achievements since the day I moved my toes!

It was important to me to show others what I could do. I wanted to be an inspiration to others that may be going through issues of their own. They could always think of that moment and tell themselves that if Keith could do that, then I can overcome my obstacle as well.

For this same reason, I have dipped my toe into the world of motivational speaking. I have spoken to elementary school groups, athletic teams and to others that are in a similar situation to me. This includes peer group meetings at Mary Free Bed. The Covid virus in early 2020 put the brakes on speaking to large groups.

Dancing At the Wedding

I had a setback in March, 2019 I was standing confidently at my walker with my arms strapped to the armrests. I had done this many times before and was not concerned about the likelihood of what was to come. My legs completely gave out and I slowly fell to the floor pulling the walker down with me. My arms were still strapped in and I felt an incredible wave of pain in my right shoulder. Above the nipple line was one of the only places I could feel pain and I got a hefty dose of it. A trip to urgent care revealed a torn bicep muscle as well as a torn muscle in my shoulder. Additionally, I had a fractured humerus which is the bone at the very top of the shoulder. Injuries in that area can't be casted so I was sent home with a sling and instructions to keep it immobile for several weeks. Bye-bye therapy. To this day that shoulder is painful. The torn bicep muscle causes a constant stinging on the inside of my elbow. Surgery to repair the damage is not practical as the level of therapy required would be painful and no long-term improvement could be guaranteed. With occupational therapy they have improved slightly but cause me to do a lot more things left-handed. I wear a lidocaine patch on my shoulder and put an over-the-counter cream, Valtaran, on my elbow to help ease the pain when needed.

I had always been somewhat ambidextrous. I golfed left-handed, I bowled left-handed. These skills helped me adapt quickly to becoming a left-handed eater, writer and texter.

In October, 2019 Sarah and I moved across the state to her hometown of Portage, just outside of Kalamazoo. Sarah realized that she was going to need some more help with me. Both of her sisters lived nearby along with six adult nieces and nephews and their spouses. We also have seven great nieces and great nephews as well. We love spending time with the kiddos. Gloria and Rich knew of a duplex available for rent. The landlord was very willing to work with us to make it more accessible for me. We had a ramp in the garage and wider doorways throughout. He even gave us the okay to put in our must have roll-in shower.

Only 10 days after moving I experienced a different kind of medical emergency. It was early morning and Sarah and I were still in bed. Sarah woke up to a gurgling sound. She looked over at me and I was in the midst of a full body seizure. I was shaking violently. She called 911 and by the time the EMTs arrived my convulsions had stopped. However, I had severe cognitive issues. I didn't know where I was. I was unresponsive. Unable to recognize or respond to anyone. Scared to death, Sarah watched as I was wheeled out to the ambulance. Once again, Sarah was allowed to spend the nights with me in the hospital.

After several days in the hospital, I didn't experience any additional seizures. I had multiple tests done on my brain. (Remarkably, they found one!) The diagnosis was transient global amnesia (TGA). Basically, this was a condition that will always be difficult to predict its onset in the future. It was likely to return, but not certain. I was put on a medication to help prevent this from happening again. The diagnosis is actually kind of handy for me. Whenever I forget to do something or if I forget something Sarah has told me I just claim "TGA". I'd like to think that this gets me off the hook. I still get these memory lapses to this day. Usually, I can tell Sarah that I am confused and she talks me through it. In just a few minutes I am back to normal. I was home alone during my most recent episode, sitting at my computer. I only remember that when I returned to normal, I had written several paragraphs of gibberish. In a weird way I was proud of myself for navigating my way through that. I still have small episodes but nothing major.

I do have large gaps in my memory. There are many things that Sarah and I have seen or done since my accident that I don't remember. An example is remembering what one of my nephew's houses looks like even though I have been there before. I can remember minute details from experiences prior to my accident, as far back as my childhood, but I can't remember everything that happened last week. Often times I have to ask Sarah if I've already asked a person a question before I text or email them the same question. TGA is a type of seizure. Please forgive me if I ask you something that you think I already know or have asked you recently. TGA!

I also spent some time in the hospital in November 2020. I was one of those statistics that had the coronavirus. I spent four days in the hospital. By far the worst part was that I spent these days without Sarah by my side. Covid had banned visitors regardless of my condition. These were the first and only nights that we have spent apart since my accident. This hospital room, understandably, was not set up for a quadriplegic. Since I couldn't use the normal call button for the nurse, they gave me a round padded button that was supposed to be easier for me to manipulate. It wasn't. At one point I didn't see my nurse for six hours. I really needed my Sarah right next to me.

Sarah did not escape Covid either. However, she did not have the luxury of leaving me alone and admitting herself to the hospital. She ended up being sick for 14 days. Our daughter-in-law, Alyson, answered the call bravely and stayed with us for over a week taking care of us. We knew that Andy had picked the right girl to marry! Sarah and I are both got the vaccination but it made both of us sick. Now, we take flu shots and pneumonia shots but we pass on the Covid vaccinations.

One of the great advantages of moving to the west side of the state is that we are less than one hour from Grand Rapids. Grand Rapids, you may recall, is the home of Mary Free Bed rehabilitation hospital. One hour seems like a long way to go for one or two hours of therapy, but this is Mary Free Bed therapy! Home sweet home!

I worked with Jake on PT. We spent the majority of our time working on standing and walking. I felt rejuvenated just wheeling in the doors. So many positive memories. So many familiar faces. Even people that I never worked with but saw in the hallways or working in the therapy room recognized Sarah and I and greeted us warmly.

One of those faces belonged to Dr. Ho. I came there, went home and have now come back but he stayed! He wasn't lying that first time I met him. Dr. Ho's office maintained my baclofen pump. He works with Amy, his nurse practitioner. She is very knowledgeable and interesting to talk to. When not working all day at MFB, she raises 1000 head of beef cattle with her husband and two daughters.

I also worked with another Amy, an OT. Her expert eye noticed that I had further damage from my earlier fall that broke my humerus. She identified my torn bicep injury as a "Popeye bicep". I assumed she was just impressed by how muscular I was. That was not the case and she explained to me that this occurs when the bicep is torn from the bone and it rolls up on itself. She tried different massage techniques to help with the pain but it still lingers.

As time passes since my accident, it has become more and more difficult to get additional therapies approved by the insurance company. Sarah is very adept at keeping diligent notes of our correspondence with various therapists, doctors and insurance representatives. Every request for renewal of my therapy leaves us holding our breath hoping that it would be approved. I would recommend to anyone to keep a detailed paper trail of dealings with insurance companies. Oftentimes they need to be reminded that they are working with an individual and not just a number on the computer screen. Overall, Sarah has had very good success in keeping the insurance approvals flowing. It is important for the service provider and the patient to work together as advocates when dealing with the insurance company. It is in their own best interest but it is in my best interest as well.

The Popeye bicep was a perfect example of this. Initially, it was difficult to get treatment approved. The best treatment to repair or at least reduce the pain of the Popeye bicep was therapy, of course. Amy didn't think she could get any additional OT therapy for me. This was more of a PT diagnosis. Jake didn't think the insurance company was likely to approve more visits since he was already working on my legs. You can see how dizzy Sarah can get from chasing her own tail.

Sarah played the game and with a separate diagnosis from our primary care physician for my shoulder injury she was able to secure PT sessions. Since everyone at MFB thought it would be difficult to get approval for these sessions there, we looked closer to home. We found a great group of people only 15 minutes from our house at Rehab Specialists. I worked with Alicia and Amy. As I have found with all of my previous therapists these two were very knowledgeable and very personable. They both had experience at Mary Free Bed, including experience with spinal cord patients.

I still wasn't getting as much therapy as I desired. One way we have been able to solve the problem of insurance approvals and inactivity was to contact a local college that has occupational therapy and physical therapy students looking to make additional money. We were very lucky to find Claire, an OT student at Western Michigan University. Claire came to our home two or three times a week to stretch me and do some strengthening exercises. We had great conversations; I get the benefit of movement and Sarah gets an hour or so to do whatever she pleases.

A favorite activity of mine to keep my arms and fingers limber is to play Trouble against myself. I am not strong enough to push the dome that holds the die, but I roll a die with my left hand and move the pieces around the board with my right (good shoulder therapy). My wrists and fingers are usually very tight at first, but by the time I am done I feel much better. Anything is better than just watching TV and remaining stagnant. Although, there is a time and place for that as well.

I can play cards using a wooden holder with lines scored along its top. The cards are placed in those lines and I am able to pinch my fingers together so that I can pull cards out of the rack and place them on the table. It becomes quite a challenge when playing a game called "65" in which each player starts with 13 cards. I am not very good at Twister though.

The earth had circled the sun for enough years (five) that I became eligible to receive a new wheelchair. My first wheelchair was a Permobil model F3. For my second chair I was able to upgrade to an F5. The exciting difference between the two models is that this chair allows me to rise up into a standing position. This is of great benefit to me. Getting weight off my bottom and putting weight through my legs and feet is an important objective. Most worrisome to Sarah is the fact that I am able to drive the chair while in that standing position. I've only gone a few feet so far but I look forward to future drives. I will now be able to give standing ovations at concerts and sporting events. Too bad for the guy sitting behind me.

The insurance company was very efficient when ordering my new chair. However, they don't pay for everything. I may as well have been buying a luxury SUV. Between insurance, self-pay and a grant from the wheelchair company my Permobil F5 wheelchair cost just north of $50,000! I am very grateful to have it.

We have a rail above my bed that allows a motor that lifts me in my sling to move across my bed. We originally got it while we were living in Grand Blanc. It has subsequently moved with us to Portage and Ohio. If not for this rail we would have to use the manual lift that I described earlier. This is much too cumbersome to move around the bedroom.

I have a hospital bed. Although certainly not as deluxe as the beds in an actual hospital it performs all of the actions that I need it to. My head and feet can be raised or lowered and the entire bed can be raised or lowered. This is important for our transfers in and out of bed. Additionally, after several bed sores we were told about a mattress that is conformed in a way that prevents bedsores much more effectively. Air constantly flows through channels in the mattress which adjusts the pressure points on my body. This eliminates the necessity of putting a pillow underneath me.

*Greatness is not measured by
what a person accomplishes,
but by the opposition that person
overcomes to reach their goals*

–Dorothy Height

CHAPTER 13
Heading South

Andy completed his residency in pharmacy at Ohio State University in July, 2019. (I believe they prefer to be addressed as THE Ohio State University but that won't be happening in this book) Initially, Alyson was working in Ann Arbor and driving to Columbus every weekend. When Covid came along it was actually a good thing for the two of them since Alyson would have to work remotely. She didn't need to be Ann Arbor so she joined Andy full-time in Columbus. Covid also required our youngest son Matthew to work remotely. He moved in with us in Portage and continued to do so when we moved to Ohio.

In July, 2020 Andy was offered a full-time position working at the cancer hospital in the OSU system, the James Hospital. They bought a house in the suburb of Dublin. We knew that grandchildren would likely be in our future and we definitely wanted to be a part of that. Shortly after the kids bought their house Sarah began the search for our next home.

We used the same realtor that Andy and Alyson did. I stayed put while Sarah made several trips south to look at houses. She finally narrowed it down to a handful and went down once again with her sisters to get their input. On September 3, 2021 we made an offer to buy a condominium in Hilliard, Ohio. This was 7 miles away from the kids but actually took 20 minutes to make the drive. (As the years passed, we realized that just about everything is 20 minutes away. We still have not figured out how that is possible) This was fortuitous timing as Andy and Alyson announced to us on my birthday, September 22, that we would soon be grandparents! We knew we were doing the right thing.

We did a virtual closing on the condo on September 27, 2021. However, there was plenty of drama yet to occur before we made the move. Right around the time we were sorting through new places to live, I was diagnosed with a severe infection in the bone of my foot just below the pinky toe. This was caused by pressure from standing on it and there wasn't enough fat to protect the bone. I had to be put on IV antibiotics. A port was put into my chest. A nurse taught Sarah how to change the antibiotic bags. This nurse came out once a week just to verify that Sarah had everything under control. As usual, Sarah did! My treatment lasted two weeks.

Ah, but the excitement continued. On October 7 while preparing things for the move, Sarah fell down the basement stairs. She was able to call 911. She knew that she had broken her ankle and it was confirmed when the paramedics arrived. These were not the most effective paramedics. Their brilliant solution to get Sarah back upstairs was to have her lift herself by her arms while they held her fragile ankle in place. She had surgery the next day. All of my caregiving couldn't just stop. Claire and Sarah's sister Gloria picked up most of the slack. I started using the sling to get in and out of bed because Sarah could no longer do the squat pivots. Friends and family started a meal train. We never had to worry about going hungry.

As Sarah healed, she jumped back into action using the phone and Internet to set me up with a new team of doctors and therapists that we would need when we arrived in Ohio. The insurance we were used to calling Blue Cross in Michigan was called Anthem. All things related to OSU medical fall under the title of the Wexner Medical Center, named after a very wealthy benefactor. They took our insurance and before we made the move Sarah already had found a primary care physician, and a physiatrist that would be able to see me. These are the two most important doctors I need.

Based on our success working with Claire, Sarah started searching for a student that could stretch me when we arrived. She also found a home healthcare agency to help us out initially until we got settled in. We had to self-pay for this as insurance did not cover it.

Things started moving quickly. Sarah had the boot removed from her foot on December 20 which would enable her to drive again. December 28 was moving day. We were moving into an over 55 community and we immediately met our sweet new neighbor Ella Mae, a 90-year-old bowler.

The condo is a 1700 square foot ranch style home with three bedrooms. Fortunately, there was already a ramp from the garage leading into the house. The door from the garage leads to a laundry room. We had a power door installed so that I could open or close the door with a remote placed on the washing machine.

The garage is a two-car but we only park the van on one side and use the other side for the space needed for using the van's ramp. We also use the other half for storage. Don't get Sarah started on what a pain in the butt that garage is. It's not your normal two-car garage. It is actually two one car garage doors that open to one large garage. The van has to be backed in because my ramp is on the passenger side. The width of the garage door is barely wide enough to get our van through. Sarah has to use the backup camera, while I try to my help with the passenger side width. Sarah has to fold in her passenger side mirror when coming or going. Once parked, she has to squeeze out her door to exit the van. Every return trip home is a stressful event! The driveway is on a steep angle and is not an option to park the van. Luckily, our condo is an end unit. I'm not too sure that the condo association is too thrilled about it but we use the two parking spots at the end of the road for Matthew's GMC Terrain and Sarah's Equinox. She drives that vehicle when I am not with her so that we can keep the mileage down on the van.

Prior to moving in, we hired a contractor to make several changes, similar to the ones we made in both residences in Michigan, that would make the condo more accessible for me. All of the doorways were widened. The door to what would become my office was completely removed. The door to the master bathroom was widened and replaced with a sliding barn door. A completely flat roll in shower was installed along with a removable showerhead.

Carpeting was pulled up in several rooms and replaced with hardwood flooring. The only exception is the guest bedroom which I have no reason to ever go into. There is a sunroom off of the main living room that we had a ramp installed so that I could enjoy it as well. That room was painted a bright yellow and soon became the dedicated playroom for our granddaughter, Luna. The cabinets in the kitchen and bathroom were dark in color so purely for aesthetic reasons these cabinets were repainted.

As we settled into our new living space, we still had to deal with our day-to-day medical needs. Before we made any appointments, Sarah set up an account in an online portal called My Chart. This is accessible to all of the medical personnel that I worked with at OSU. We did the same thing in Michigan but it was rarely used by the physicians there. We soon found out that this system was a valuable resource and faithfully used by the medical teams at OSU. On several occasions, test results were posted to My Chart before we had even returned home from the procedure.

The first doctor we met with was my physiatrist, Dr. Bavishi. She was referred to us by my physiatrist in Michigan. She saw us on time so that put her in the plus column right away. She was already familiar with some of my background that Sarah had entered into My Chart. All of my medications, information about my baclofen pump and other items. Dr. Bavishi's office would be taking over the maintenance of my baclofen pump. She spent a good deal of time with us as we got to know each other. She was very knowledgeable and very nice. We left her office pleased and still enjoy her care to this day.

My primary care physician is Dr. Eiterman. Sarah was his patient before I was. He had just started his practice and was accepting new patients. If you have ever tried to get into a PCP for the first time, you know how lucky we were to find him. He was very young looking. So young that I couldn't help but ask him his age. He too was familiar with my history because of the information we had already provided. He is very open to suggestions that we make about my care. Since I get so many UTIs he has given us a supply of containers to take a sample to the lab when that occurs.

We weren't in Ohio for very long until I made my first of many trips to the wound clinic where I saw Nancy. She is a Certified Nurse Practitioner. NPs are not considered "doctors" but they are able to write prescriptions. Nancy got my sense of humor so we got along right away. Unfortunately, I see her quite often. Actually, she sees me. I look back over my shoulder as she is examining the sores on my backside. Her nursing staff measures the size and depth of the wounds. (Sarah is sure to record these numbers in her notebook). Most visits she has to debride the wound. This is a process of scraping away the dead skin to make way for new skin to grow. It is quite painful and usually knocks me out for the day. During one of my visits, she wondered if instead of my sores being caused to from my bed, she wondered if my wheelchair might be causing me issues as well.

I have a Roho brand cushion on my chair which is a series of rubber fingers filled with air. To make sure that the seat was providing the necessary support she ordered a procedure called seat mapping. I was put in a sling and lifted off the chair enough so they could put a pad underneath me. Next, I was lowered back onto my chair, the sling was removed and I was moved into my normal seating area. The seat map looked similar to a weather map. By that I mean the areas where the most pressure on the cushion were red or orange. Low pressure areas were different shades of blue. The cushion has four different chambers in which to pump air. Air was either added or taken out of each quadrant to provide the best support.

Soon after my wheelchair cushion was properly set we needed a new van. Since we had moved to Ohio, we needed to find a dealer that specialized in vehicles that required aftermarket adjustments. We were referred to a company called Mobility Works. In February 2022 we put in our order for a sleek looking black Chrysler Pacifica. We received the van four weeks later and joined the hundreds of people that have horror stories from their visits to the Department of Motor Vehicles.

We simply wanted to get a handicap license plate for our van. We were told that they don't issue those even though we had already seen several vehicles with state of Ohio handicap plates on them. Their suggestion was to hang a placard from our rearview mirror even though we knew it was illegal to drive with the placard hanging in the way. That entire debacle was not resolved until we had Dr. Bavishi write a second note of necessity for us and we got into the line of a clerk that was familiar with the process. We decided to get personalized plates. Sarah decided that her grandchildren were going to call her Gigi. I wanted to be called Pop-pop. Mission accomplished! After three months of frustration our new license plate finally arrived "POPNGIGI".

GiGi and Pop-Pop you are asking. Did I miss a page? When was the grandchild born? Sorry about that. I was on a roll with the license plate story. Luna Marie Stone was born on 4/24/22. She is absolutely perfect even though she was born at Ohio State University

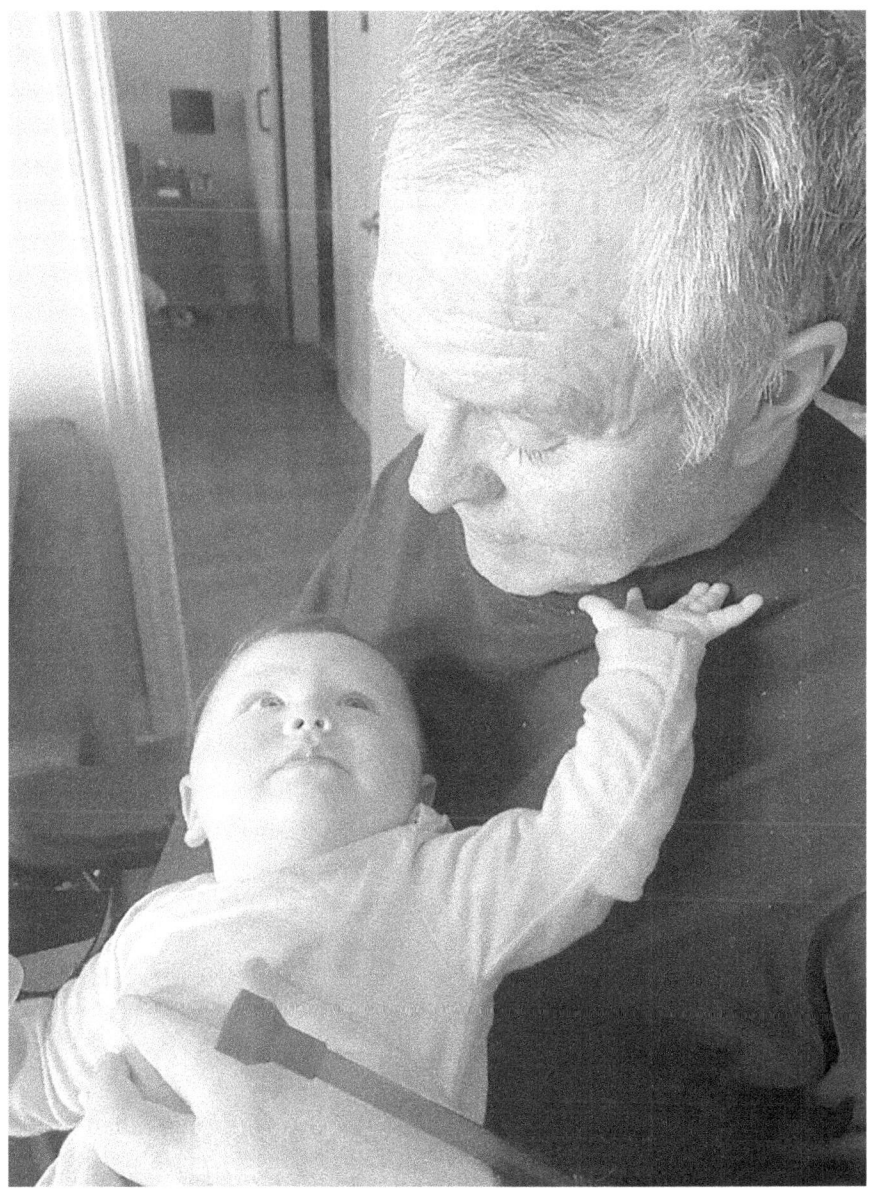

The beginning is the most important part of the work

– Plato

CHAPTER 14

Ups and Downs

We fell in love with Luna immediately. Seeing Luna made me realize how fortunate I was to still be alive so that I could meet her. God's plan that had changed things for Sarah and I almost six years ago was continuing. Watching Sarah, GiGi, hold our granddaughter was an incredible sight. Through all of the difficult times we had gone through, Luna was a bright light that made everything great.

We spend as much time as possible with Luna. I'm sure Alyson gets tired of us continually asking for a visit but that does not stop us. I am actually glad that Luna will always know her Pop-Pop as I am now, in a wheelchair. I think the transition would have been difficult if our interactions suddenly changed. Watching Andy in his new role as a father is an incredible sight. Sarah and I couldn't wait to see what was next for sweet Luna.

We had a session with the assistive technology center at OSU to go over various devices that would make my life a bit easier. Unlike all of my medically necessary equipment that I had to have, none of the devices we discussed that day were things that insurance would pay for. After talking with the OSU people, we turned our attention to the geek squad at a well-known big-box store. We already had a device to control our main TV but we added others for controlling lights and the thermostat. In total we have four devices listening to us in our house. They needed different names and the company that makes them has given their customers limited options on what to call them. Two of them on opposite ends of the house are Alexa. We summon the device in the main room as Echo. Computer is the name of the helper in our bedroom. You would be surprised how many times a computer is referenced on a TV show. It's humorous although frustrating when our device comes to life when this happens awaiting a command. I'm not a conspiracy theorist (although I do write books about them) but I have no doubt that these devices listen to us every day.

July, 2022 was a terrible month for me, health-wise. I had developed a UTI that had become so bad that I had to be taken by ambulance to the ER. I developed sepsis, which in my case meant bacteria in my blood. That's not good, to say the least. I also had ileus which meant that nothing was moving through my gastric tract. An infectious disease department was added to my care team. I was put on continuous antibiotics. I was still feeling like crap but after 48 hours later of treatment the hospital staff determined that I was healthy enough to move into a two-person room. However, this meant that Sarah could not stay in my room overnight. Having gone through it once before I knew how difficult it was going to be.

After several days, neither Sarah nor I felt I was getting better. I was throwing up bile. This was a new sensation for me. I hadn't vomited since my accident. My diaphragm was still weak so I had difficult throwing up. To work around this an NG tube was inserted through my nose. This was extremely uncomfortable for me. Without Sarah, I needed to be able to summon a nurse if I needed something. I was unable to push the regular call button. Just as my previous hospital stay, a pad was put on my chest and the plan was for me to push it with my chin. And just like my previous hospital stay, this did not work very successfully and I was often laying there alone with my thoughts.

My roommate was famous at one time, it would be more accurate to call him infamous. He was former Ohio State quarterback Art Schlichter. He was the last quarterback to play for legendary coach Woody Hayes. He was a four-year starter and is third on the list of OSU rankings for most passing yards in a career. He finished in the top 6 of Heisman voting three times. He was drafted as the fourth overall pick in the 1982 NFL draft. What hadn't been discovered yet was Schlichter's love for gambling. He had gambled away his entire $350,000 signing bonus by the middle of his first season. He got into further trouble with the kind of people you don't want to get in trouble with. In 1983 he had lost an additional $489,000. Threatened with harm from the people to whom he owed six figures to, he turned himself into the FBI and told them everything he knew. As part of his plea deal, he spent 10 years in prison.

After his release, Schlichter's focus turned to drugs. He had been arrested in Hilliard for cocaine possession just one month prior to becoming my roommate. Sarah spoke with him and he taught continuously about how much he loved his mother. By Sarah's count, he called her at least five times during the time she was there. He asked Sarah about me and told her that he wanted to talk to me. Out of his earshot she asked if I had ever heard of him. I told her I had but I was in no condition to have a coherent conversation with him.

The last Sarah saw of him, he was removing his IV as he told her he was going home to see his mother. Schlichter's most recent brush with the law was in 2024, two years after Sarah and I had the pleasure of his company. Obviously, none of Sarah's kindness rubbed off on him.

The final tally on his professional football career included four years and 13 starts in the NFL all with the Colts. One year in the Canadian Football League and finally four years in the Arena football league. He is considered to be one of the five worst draft picks in NFL history.

Looking back, perhaps my biggest regret to date, other than the accident, was that I was too ill to talk with him. I found out later that he had written a book about his life. Maybe we could have been author buddies! Amuse yourself by looking up his Wikipedia page sometime.

I had recovered enough that the hospital was ready to discharge me. They wanted to refer me to a skilled nursing facility. Sarah dismissed that option immediately and they trained her how to administer my IV antibiotics at home. Yet another task piled on to my amazing wife.

A few weeks later I was due to get my baclofen pump replaced. It needed to be replaced due to the reduction in battery life. While talking to Dr. Bavishi about that procedure she suggested that I receive Botox treatments. I thought that would be great! Even though I was a quadriplegic I would still like to look young and vibrant. Turns out I had the name right but it is used for a variety of different treatments. In my case it would be injected into my pectoral muscles to help ease their tightness. I also started to get Botox injections in my quadriceps and my forearms. They work marginally well for me and I still get them every three months. Sarah had been receiving Botox injections for her migraine headaches for quite some time.

In October, 2022 we were able to find another student, Rylee, to help with my stretching and other care for four hours a day. She attended OSU and was on a track to get into a physician's assistant program. She was from Cincinnati but she would be living in the Columbus area until she graduated in May, 2024. Just like Claire, Rylee and I spent many hours discussing issues other than my injury. My most recent book, "Dead Ball:

The Pickleball Murder", was hatched because of her love for the game of pickleball. We were able to meet her family when we went to a Detroit Tigers game in Cincinnati versus the Reds. Another medical professional met and another friend for life made. She has been accepted into the physician's assistant (PA) program at Ohio University-Cincinnati and will earn her degree in May, 2027.

The remainder of 2022 was fairly quiet for me but in September, Matthew found Sarah laying on the floor with intense stomach pain. He went with her to the hospital via ambulance. She took several tests including an endoscopy and colonoscopy. Her pain was diagnosed as an inflamed liver and spleen due to the effects Covid. A normal person would have been laid up for quite a while but Sarah was back taking care of me in just a few days. Once again, she amazed me with her physical and mental prowess.

We were excited to host Luna's first Christmas eve. We have boxes and boxes of Christmas decorations and Sarah was certain to put every one of them out. It was especially important to her to do that since we did not use them at all in 2021 because we were in the process of moving. Luna was now eight months old and just like most eight-month-olds, she was more interested in the bright lights and crinkly paper.

Winter in Ohio is only slightly better than winter in Michigan. We were both feeling pretty well when the calendar turned to 2023 so in January we headed down to Florida, stopped for a short time to visit my parents and then we continued on to make the trip through the Florida Keys all the way to Key West. It is a 94-mile drive from the beginning of the keys, Key Largo to the southernmost tip, Key West. Sarah is definitely not a fan of bridges and this trip included many. However, they were very low to the water and she was less afraid than going over a high bridge such as the Ambassador Bridge in Detroit. We had the usual spots which included Jimmy Buffett's bar and a picture by the oversized buoy that denotes this point is the southernmost in the contiguous United States. We headed back north, stayed a few days with my parents then returned home. We were pleased that I was able to sit in the van for that length of time and not develop any sores.

Another month, another UTI, another admission to the hospital. I always have bacteria in my urine because of the suprapubic catheter. My urine tests always come back dirty. We can tell the difference between a normal infection and a troublesome one by a high fever and my lack of ability to think clearly. An idea was floated that perhaps my bladder was getting infected due to my messy bowel movements. They were happening quite often and fecal matter would often be wet and end up everywhere. The infectious disease team suggested I consider a colostomy bag to capture all of the output.

I had always been opposed to having a colostomy bag for aesthetic reasons and because I felt it would made me feel older and weak. After much persuasion by my team, including Sarah, I reconsidered. I also watched several hours of YouTube videos made by other paraplegics on what a miracle they felt it was for them and the ease in which it could be cared for. Finally, in May I agreed to have the procedure done. The end of my lower intestine is directed away from my anus and into a bag attached to my abdomen. This is on the right side of my body just below where my urine catheter is inserted.

Almost immediately, I wished I had done this procedure years ago! What a difference this has made in my daily life!! I think everyone should have a colostomy bag. I can feel the sensation of a bowel movement happening but there is no longer any reason for panic. When the bag is removed, the very end of my gastric tract, which is called a stoma is visible. The stoma needs wiped just like an able-bodied person wipes after a bowel movement.

However, the odor does not go away. My shit still stinks! The bag usually needs changed once a day. Sarah does that while I am in bed. It is thrown away in the garbage. Close your eyes and imagine a hot July day with several days of my output cooking away while waiting to be taken to the dump. I'll pause here to give you a chance to run to the bathroom.

Sarah does her best to reduce the odor in our bedroom by spraying a product called "Poo-pourri". Occasionally she has to use a different product called "POOF". I am not making this up. I believe the latter product is advertised on TV. Be sure to pay attention.

I'm not done yet. Another fun fact is that the colostomy bag has a vent so that I can audibly fart. You'll remember how important that was to me when I was in the rehab hospital. Unfortunately, I cannot fart on demand. It is possible that I could let one go at any time. There have been no embarrassing problems yet but it's still early!

Knowing that Rylee would someday leave for graduate school, I needed someone to continue in her place. Sarah was talking to a therapist virtually, working through the stress of taking care of me. She was especially stressed out that I would be losing one of my lifelines. The therapist knew of a woman who had worked with homebound people similar to myself in the past. In September, 2023 we welcomed a new member to my in-home care team, Ali. Her workload had dwindled and she was looking for more clients. God had stepped in again and answered our prayers.

Rylee and I had less opportunity to work together as she prepared for her next move into graduate school. Ali stepped in immediately to fill that void. Ali is older than Claire or Rylee so she understands all my references to older movies and catchphrases from movies and TV in the 80s. She seemed to know every actor's name and what other shows they were in. She works with me for four hours a day for as many days per week that my schedule would allow. She was always available but doctor's appointments often altered our schedule.

We spend the first the first two hours of each session stretching my legs and my arms. While doing this we would also have one eye on the TV watching the latest series on one of the streaming channels. The next two hours are spent playing games which help me improve the pinching techniques of my fingers. Our favorite card games are gin or is it gin rummy? Regardless of its name we both play by the same rules. I taught her a game that I learned from Sarah's uncle George called "Kings in the Corner". We also play Scrabble. Our games were very competitive. Initially, I won most of the Scrabble games. Unfortunately for me, I taught her well and she regularly turns the table on me.

We invented a variation of Scrabble that we call "10 tiles". Each player starts with 10 tiles rather than the normal seven but the twist is that every word played must be at least four letters long. If you can't make a four-letter word using the existing tiles, a player can start their own word anywhere on the board but they do not get credit for double or triple letters/words. As the tiles run out a player is only required to play a word with one less letter than they have. For example, if you have four tiles you only have to play a three-letter word. Quick! Someone call Parker Brothers!

2023 closed out with one more surgery. The sore under my toe was not getting any better. There was no fat between my bone and skin. It was determined that I should have the bone removed from my toe to eliminate the continuous infections I was getting. The surgeon recommended that he cut a small incision in the Achilles tendon in both legs to help loosen them. It was almost impossible for me to point my toes downward before the surgery. The surgery was successful. After this procedure I wore boots at night to help the healing. Ah but things rarely go perfectly and the boots caused sores on my heels. Nancy, my wound care expert, recommended that we stop using the boots. I did and the sores healed after several months.

Our greatest glory is not in never falling but in rising up every time we fall

– Emerson

CHAPTER 15
Welcome to the World, Eli

The calendar turned to 2024. Nancy took another look at my wounds and she determined that it was okay for Sarah and I to travel to Florida for some warm weather and to visit my parents. We rented a condo closer to Orlando because Andy, Alyson and Luna were also coming down for one week. My health started to deteriorate just as the kids were leaving to fly back to Michigan. The wounds on my backside had returned with a vengeance. I stayed in bed for two days. Sarah took pictures of my sores and sent them to Nancy. We surmised that because I used a normal mattress rather than the airflow mattress that I described earlier these areas became irritated once again. Rather than spending another night on a hotel mattress that could irritate the sores further, Sarah drove 14 hours directly home to get me back into my own bed since it was better for the sores. We saw Nancy the morning after we arrived home and it only took one quick look at the sores before she immediately admitted me to the hospital.

I had a Magnetic Resonance Image (MRI) done which for most people is not a big deal. However, the magnets used in an MRI machine shuts down my baclofen pump. The test had to be scheduled around the availability of a technician that could restart my pump upon completion.

The MRI confirmed our worst fears. The infection had gotten into my bone. This would require another round of IV antibiotics. Sarah was retrained on how to administer the antibiotic. She had already had to do this in 2021. After receiving six days of treatment in the hospital I was released. I had a very regimented schedule when I returned home.

At 5 AM, 9:30 AM, 2 PM and 9 PM the IV antibiotics were administered. Each IV took about 30 minutes to complete. I also took an oral antibiotic with my morning pills. Sarah changed the dressing on my wounds every morning as well. Throughout the day, even though I had the new mattress, Sarah rolled me from one side or the other every 20 minutes. Sarah also had to use a contraption called a "wound vacuum". It was put on the wound several times a day and its purpose was to literally vacuum out debris and dead tissue from my wound so that new healthy tissue could grow in its place. This process continued for 12 weeks. A registered nurse came to our house once a week to confirm that everything was going as planned. We were seeing Nancy quite often depending on the condition of my wounds. While I Was on the IV, I couldn't get my Botox shots because it is a toxin. The antibiotics recognize the Botox as an invasion of my body and they attack it which makes the procedure in effective.

To prevent bed sores while we travel, we have purchased a portable mattress topper that we take when we travel. It uses the same technology as the mattress I use at home.

I was referred to a sports medicine doctor to see if I could get some relief from my shoulder pain. He recommended cortisone shots and they work very well for a couple months at a time. More recently, I have been getting the cortisone shots on the inside of my elbow which also helped. I continue to get those to date.

On 5/19/24 we welcomed Eli Parker Stone into our family! Luna was now a big sister. I love Luna so much that I wasn't sure if I had enough love to give another grandchild. What a ridiculous thought! The moment I looked into his dark blue eyes I found an abundance of love in my heart for him and the rest the people in my life. As the weeks go by his peach fuzz hair and eyebrows were coming in red just like his father's. He has a wonderful smile that he flashes often. Also, like his father, he has a dimple on one side. I thank God every day that I am still here to spend time with him and his sister.

Somehow, Luna had become a toddler. One of my favorite parts of my life is watching Sarah with Luna. She started spending longer periods of time at our house. She has even had a couple of sleepovers. She loves grabbing her GiGi's finger and leading her around to play with the multitude of toys and books we have collected. Our house has a separate room, painted yellow, where we spend most of our time with her. Luna alternates playing with a dollhouse, a Minnie Mouse and Daisy Duck tea party set (Daisy seems to spill a lot of tea), a pretend grocery store including a shopping cart and of course several toys with bright lights and loud noises. Being a lifelong elementary school educator, Sarah has always had an extensive collection of children's books and Luna loves to hear a good story. Sometimes they read while sitting on a small couch covered with scenes from Frozen. Other times they leave the yellow room and read on the couch in the family room. There is a small ramp leading from the family room into the yellow room so I am also able to play with them.

Lunch with Luna usually consists of "mick mouse mac & cheese", grapes or raspberries and yogurt. That girl is quite a chatterbox and her Gigi and I love listening to her stories. Even while she is lying down for her nap, we can hear her talking to her favorite stuffed animal, bunbun, for quite some time before she surrenders and falls asleep. She brings us so much joy!

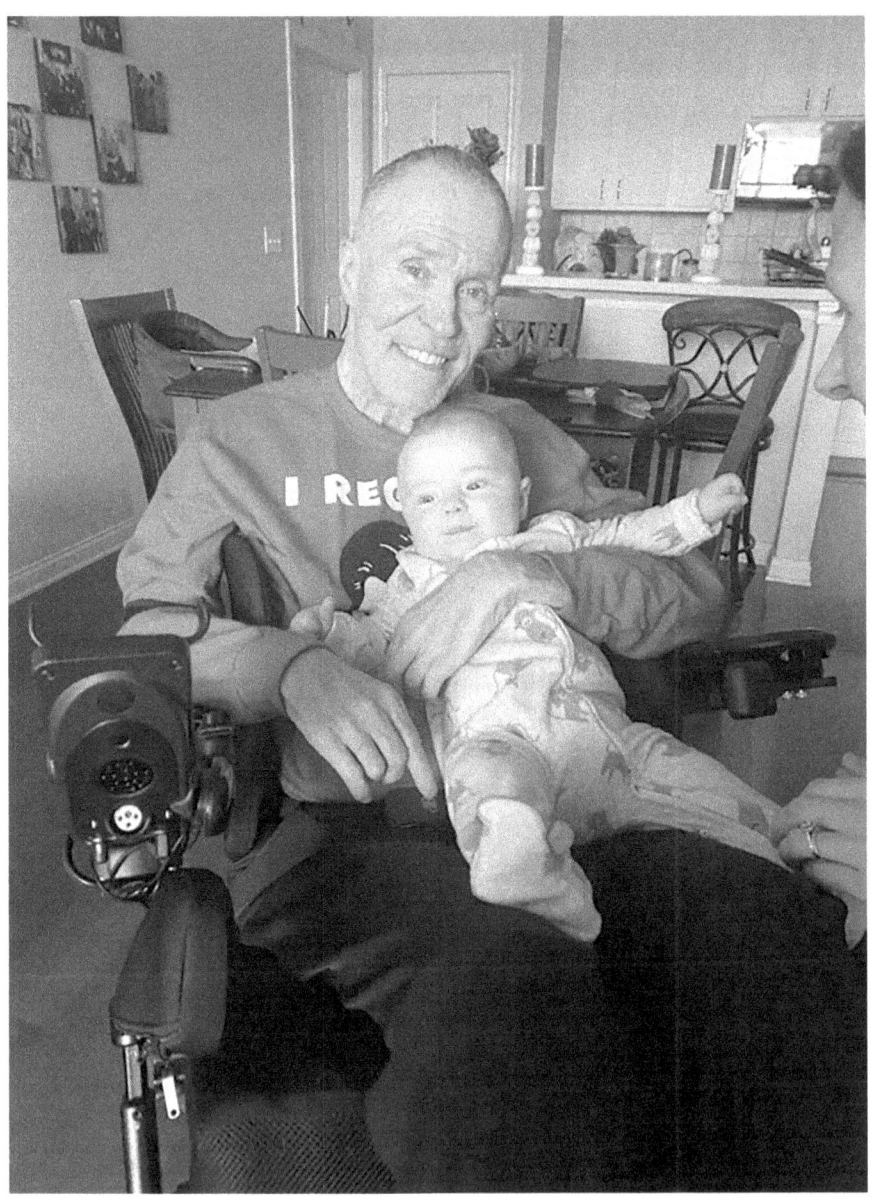

Soon, Eli will be part of playtime as well. He is already pulling himself up to stand and crawling at a world-class pace. Andy and Alyson have their hands full with the two of them and they wouldn't have it any other way.

Shortly after Eli was born, I started having trouble with swallowing and talking. I also could not get a deep breath. I started losing a considerable amount of weight, 40 pounds since February. No one had to tell me that a cause for the sudden loss of weight could be cancer. I was the only one that ever said the "C" word. I was at my lowest point. I could hardly talk and every breath was labored. I felt so poorly that my mood had soured. I told Sarah I wished they would find cancer and when they did, I would not treat it. I didn't want to be a burden on anyone anymore.

I was given a litany of tests. I had an ultrasound done of my kidneys and gallbladder. I had some stones in each but not enough to be the cause of any weight loss. Cancer was ruled out. I had CT scans done of my entire abdomen. Everything was normal.

I had a lung function test which led to a diagnosis that my diaphragm had become weak through the years which inhibited my ability to take a good breath. I still felt like crap but I was starting to rethink my desire for a cancer diagnosis.

I had an endoscopy to examine my esophagus. Esophageal cancer was the cancer that killed my friend Jeff that you read about way back in chapter 1. Again, there were no signs of cancer but I was diagnosed with lymphocytic esophagitis. In a nutshell, this diagnosis meant that I had a problem with the flaps that covered my esophagus which is why I had difficulty swallowing.

Allow me to take a minute to offer a hearty congratulations to the pharmaceutical industry! During my endoscopy, I was given a drug called Propanol which put my body into something called "conscious sedation". It's the same drug I was given for my colonoscopy when I turned 50. All I remember from the procedure is laying on my side, having a mouthpiece inserted and being told "good night". My next recollection is waking up in recovery which I believe was 20 minutes later. There were no aftereffects whatsoever. I'm pretty sure this is the drug that Michael Jackson got addicted to. He may have tried other drugs besides Propanol but nothing "beat it". See what I did there?

This diagnosis brought a new therapist into my life. William was a speech therapist and he worked with me on diaphragmatic breathing exercises. For example, I would inhale as deeply as possible and then exhale while vocalizing "eeeeee" for as long as I could. At first, I could only do that for three seconds. William demonstrated that normally that exhale should last 20 to 30 seconds. I saw him twice a week and did the exercises with Ali and Sarah as well.

On a daily basis, I use a device called a spirometer. This is a tool to help me increase my lung capacity. I inhale as deeply as possible and a plastic disc floats up the side of the spirometer. Basically, it is a visual way for me to see my lung capacity. I also use a plastic device we call a "pickle" because it looks like, well, a pickle. With this device I inhale through my nose and exhale as powerfully as I can through my mouth. The circumference of the tube inside the pickle can be adjusted making it more difficult for me to push air through.

As part of my treatment for the lymphocytic esophagitis I was referred to a doctor to examine my vocal cords. He put a camera down my throat and Sarah and I saw some amazing pictures of my vocal cords. They had atrophied a great deal and did not close completely over my esophagus. He knew exactly what he had to do. He numbed my vocal cords and as we watched he inserted a needle down my throat and injected my vocal cords with a steroid gel. Right before my eyes I watched my vocal cords plump up and completely close over my esophagus. I was able to take deeper breaths almost immediately. However, I could not speak. This was expected and would continue for the next several days. She never said it out loud but I'm sure Sarah enjoyed not hearing any smart-ass comments from me for a while. Believe it or not, I think you are all caught up regarding my medical history. I hope to return to outpatient therapy and doing some more walking. That part of my life has lagged far behind. Time to get back to work!

Attitude and effort are the only things you can control

—Billy Cox

CHAPTER 16
Out of the House

It is important for our mental health that Sarah and I get out of the house and try to lead as normal a life as possible. Part of that is to continue to attend events that we had always enjoyed in the past. Our first large-scale event was Matthew's graduation from the University of Michigan. The graduation was held at Crisler Center. There were no reserved seats and we were a bit nervous about finding a spot for my wheelchair. It turned out to be quite easy. The seats set aside for wheelchairs were higher up in the arena since I couldn't traverse down the stairs. It was set up so that there was an empty space for my wheelchair with a folding chair beside it for a companion. Sarah sat next to me while other family members sat in arena seats near us.

The event with the greatest amount of people that we have attended so far was an Ed Sheeran concert at Ford Field with 50,000 of our closest friends. I had a couple of fears when we discussed going to this event. The first was quickly dismissed as I was able to find tickets on an aftermarket site, in this case I used Stub Hub. One of the items on ticket purchasing sites that you may have ever noticed is the filter section. Through the filter I am able to slide a button to show only handicap accessible seating.

Of course, this narrows down my options considerably but I am happy with how easy it is to navigate.

The other thing we have to deal with at these events is parking. Handicap parking spots are always available. This was the case at the Ford Field parking garage. Sarah had to stick the nose of the van into a spot clear of the vehicle parked next to and lower the ramp so that I could get out. We perform this mover as fast as possible in consideration of the people behind us. It has always seemed to work out for us. Our return to the car after the concert, however, proved to be a bit more difficult but comical. The gates at the booth where we paid when we entered the parking garage were down and there were no personnel on site. There was a sidewalk but no ramp for me to access it. After a few minutes of mental problem-solving we decided to play a party game; LIMBO! We sized up the bar and agreed that if I laid completely flat in my wheelchair, I should be able to get under the bar. I lowered my head all the way back and made sure that the height of the wheelchair was as low as possible. Cue the calypso music and soon I was on the other side of the bar!

One of the Griswolds, Pat Donnelly, arranged for tickets to a Red Wings hockey game for us. Similar to the Sheeran concert, the most stressful part of the evening was finding a parking spot. The seats for the game were excellent. We sat at the top of the lower bowl of seats which were about 25 rows from the ice. Similar to our set up at Michigan there was a companion seat next to the opening for my wheelchair so that Sarah and I could sit next to each other. No limbo or any other kind of gymnastics were required to exit.

Pat Donnelly, by way of his sister, came through again and got a suite at a Detroit Tigers game. The suite came with a parking pass that the Griswolds generously gave to us. Living the high life in a suite could easily spoil me. It was very easy to get around. We took an elevator to the suite level. This was a carefree outing with no parking worries and plenty of room to get around the suite. It was a great day to spend with two dozen of my best friends.

Sarah and I have also attended a Tigers spring training game in Lakeland, Florida. I'm not sure if it was due to the older population or what the reason but there was plentiful handicapped parking. Similar to all the other venues I have described, Sarah sat in a regular seat and I pulled in next to her in my wheelchair.

In 2019, we went to an outdoor concert venue at Soaring Eagle Casino in Mount Pleasant, Michigan to see one of Sarah's all-time favorites, Tim McGraw. We stayed at the casino so there were no parking issues. However, I did have to drive my wheelchair across a vast gravel parking lot to get to the venue. All of that bouncing and jostling cause me to spasm and get very tight. I was eventually able to loosen up in a short period of time. Xanax is very helpful for that! Our seats were very close to the front. At one point Sarah even got to reach out and touch McGraw's hand. Not just once but a second time as well. I cannot confirm nor deny whether she has washed it since.

It's not uncommon for people to unknowingly walk in front of my path. I don't suppose they think to look that low. However, that night I profited from one of those encounters. After the McGraw concert we were going back across the gravel lot towards the hotel when an inebriated concertgoer walked right into me. He was very apologetic and reached into his pocket and handed me a $20 bill along with another apology. We tried to give it back but he wouldn't hear of it. You don't need to tell me twice. I kept the money planning to double it at the casino.

One of my therapists at Level 11, Luis, had told me he would be at the concert as well. He found us. It was nice to spend some time with him outside the gym. Knowing someone at an event we went to was not uncommon. Sarah would often let people know via Facebook when we were going somewhere. We have had visitors at several of our outings. She liked the idea of having backup in case it was needed. As always, Sarah's connections came through. It's great to have supportive people nearby!

Now that I had $20 burning a hole in my pocket we headed for the casino. My game of choice is blackjack. All of the blackjack tables are similar to high-tops at a restaurant. With some maneuvering, I probably could have pulled into one of the spots. However, what you may have never noticed before is that casinos have lower handicap accessible tables as well. They are scarce but they do exist. There are no heavy chairs to move out of the way and I was able to pull in to one of the positions all of which are wider than a normal table set up. The beauty of blackjack is that the player is only allowed to touch their chips. No touching of the cards. I can move my arms so I was able to make the required hand gestures for the benefit of the "eye in the sky" cameras. As I got fatigued, Sarah was allowed to handle my chips. Disappointingly, there were no extra aces in the deck for a quadriplegic. My $20 bill along with several others disappeared into the dealer's vault.

We have attended two Michigan State University basketball games at the Breslin Center with tremendously different experiences. Our first game in December, 2017 went as expected, similar to all of our other experiences. Again, we sat just behind the top of the lower section, Sarah in a companion seat and me next to her in my wheelchair.

We returned for another game in December, 2019. While we were still in the area just above the lower section, this time there was yellow tape on the floor in the shape of boxes. All of these boxes were in the same row. Behind them was a row of folding chairs. We found out that these were the companion seats. Sarah had to sit behind me which made conversation very difficult and her view was almost completely blocked by my wheelchair. Sarah went to customer service and only got a promise of a phone call to explain the new policy the next day. No phone call ever came.

I felt the need to investigate as to what had happened since 2017. I reached out to the Lansing State Journal and they did an article about my situation with no comment from MSU. I was also scheduled to do an interview with a Lansing television station. After a week of correspondence back and forth with the TV station, I received an email from the reporter telling me that after talking to MSU officials, they would no longer be pursuing the story. I asked for an explanation but never received it. I then took my questions directly to MSU. I looked up the ADA laws on the government website www.ada.gov. The law clearly states "people purchasing a ticket for an accessible seat may purchase up to 3 additional seats for companions in the *same row* and the seats must be contiguous with the accessible seat".

Here are the highlights of the email I finally received, (11 days after the game) from the ADA coordinator at Michigan State University, Aislinn Sapp. "... Let me say how truly sorry I am that your experience at the Breslin Center did not meet your expectations. ADA accessibility is very important to MSU and we consistently are working to ensure accessibility on campus. We are committed to creating and maintaining a physical environment that is as accessible and user-friendly as possible, so I am sorry to hear about the difficulties you and your wife encountered during your recent visit. I wanted to try and address some of the specific concerns that you raised about the accessible seating at the Breslin Center. The building standards that you referenced in your email" (this is the information I found regarding that companion seats should be in the same row as the handicapped seat) "appear to be the ADA 2010 standards (they were). Those standards apply to buildings that have been constructed and/or renovated since March, 2012. The Breslin Center was constructed in 1989 and the seating arena has not been renovated since the 2010 standards were enacted. Thus, the Breslin Center is not subject to the standards you likely found at ADA.gov. The Breslin Center meets all building codes, including with respect to accessible seating. Please be assured that even though the Breslin Center is fully compliant with all relevant building codes we are taking your experience and your feedback very seriously."

Basically, I got a pat on the head and was politely told to go away. I responded by relating my completely different experience only two years earlier. I did my research and discovered that in 2017 there were renovations done at Breslin including widening of the corridors which are connected to the seating platforms where the wheelchair seating is located. I pointed this out in one of my subsequent emails. I never received any further communication from the University. Nor have I ever returned for another game. We talked to others sitting around us at the 2019 game and we were told by a couple with season tickets that the change had occurred the previous year. They were more upset that their seating area was not consistent. They sat in a different place for each game. You are better than that MSU.

With the exception of MSU, we have had pleasant experiences at all of the venues we have attended. If I don't find a link online for handicapped accessible seating, I call the box office directly and purchase tickets that way. Since my accident we have attended baseball games in Detroit, Pittsburgh, Cleveland and Cincinnati. All without any difficulty. It has become an annual tradition to meet the Gielarowskis at a Tigers game in different nearby cities. That's how we ended up going to games in Pittsburgh and Cleveland. We try to stay within a reasonable driving distance. Future venues on our radar are the two stadiums in Chicago for the Cubs and the White Sox and the Brewers in Milwaukee. Milwaukee has a dome so that should be nice. Day games are best for Sarah and I. She does not like driving in the dark especially in an area that we know nothing about. For the games when we meet the Gielarowskis we stay within walking/wheeling distance of the stadiums. This is more expensive but it is well worth it for the convenience.

Sarah and I have flown one time; from my parent's home in Florida back to Michigan for a close friend's wedding in 2019. Anything with a battery makes the airlines nervous. The heavy power wheelchair would have to be stowed in the belly of the plane with the luggage. I can't get comfortable with that idea. The instructions on the airlines website also suggested to attach a copy of the wheelchair owner's manual in case the chair needed to be disassembled for any reason. Disassembled? I wasn't going to take that chance. Since it was only a weekend trip the best course of action would be to take my manual wheelchair without the battery-powered wheels. This meant that Sarah would have to push me everywhere I went. It also meant that I would not have the ability for pressure relief. Both of these things made me nervous. I don't think I will ever be much of an airline traveler. We have not looked into renting a wheelchair but I suppose that is a possibility. We are open to suggestions.

My parents dropped us off at the airport with plenty of time to spare. We had always given ourselves plenty of time to get to airports even before my accident, but we were even more cognizant of it now. Sitting around at the gate, the usual announcements began. It was the first chance I had to take advantage of the opportunity to be an early boarder. A flight attendant met us on the ramp just in front of the door to the plane. I had to transfer from my wheelchair into a much narrower chair so that I could get down the aisle with ease. Our seats were located in the first row of coach just behind first class. We were fortunate as these seats are not necessarily reserved for people like me. The extra legroom was much appreciated. Sarah and a flight attendant lifted me into my seat and the wheelchair was stowed in the forward cabin. It was the first time in quite a while that I wasn't sitting in my wheelchair. It was a nice change. The flight went smoothly. We waited patiently after landing and we were the last to deplane. The flight attendant brought the small wheelchair to my seat and the process was reversed. Airplane seat to small wheelchair, up the aisle to the jetway and finally small wheelchair to my manual chair.

Andy met us at the airport driving an accessible van we had rented for the weekend. Sarah strapped me in and we returned to our home in Grand Blanc.

Everything went perfectly. The wedding was beautiful. Sarah and I were able to see lots of friends that we hadn't seen in a while. The lack of frequent pressure releases didn't seem to cause any harm. Often times, Sarah would just tilt me back and hold the chair for short periods. At the wedding we recruited volunteers for the job giving me time to talk to a group of people while Sarah was able to talk to a different group in another location. Sarah got a good workout from pushing me around as well, whether she wanted it or not.

After two nights in Michigan, we flew back to Florida, again without incident, repeating the actions we took for the previous flight. My parents picked us up in our van and we returned to their house. Sarah seemed happier than usual to transfer me back into my power chair.

Since that flight, Sarah has read about the possibility of Delta Airlines putting docking stations for wheelchairs into their planes. If this comes to fruition without an exorbitant price, this might get us to places we might not ordinarily go. We will be keeping our eyes on this development.

Don't tell anyone but Sarah turned 60 in December, 2024. To celebrate that milestone birthday, she wanted to take the immediate family on a Disney cruise. We went in January so that the grandchildren would still be home when Santa came to visit. Luna was 2 ½ years old and infatuated by the princesses. Sarah had planned this for over a year and could not wait. Since flying is a no go for me, Sarah and I drove down early and spent 10 bonus days with my parents.

The Disney ship, Fantasy, was scheduled to leave on a Sunday at 3 PM from Port Canaveral, Florida. Matthew, Andy, Alyson, Luna & Eli flew to Orlando one day prior and took a Disney provided shuttle to the ship. Sarah and I boarded the ship at noon. We went to our state room first to check it out. Our luggage wouldn't arrive until later. The handicap accessible room was at the very front of the ship. Our porthole window looked directly over the bow of the ship. There was plenty of room for me to maneuver the wheelchair around the room. The bathroom shower had no lip making access for me would have been very easy. We did not lug my shower chair onto the ship. It was sponge-baths and no rinse shampoo for me.

Matthew shared our room and slept on the couch. Andy's family stayed just around the corner from us. There was a significant difference between the widths of the entry doors to our cabin and theirs. There was no way to get my wheelchair into that room. It made us even more thankful for the room we had.

If you have ever been on a cruise, you are aware that before the ship leaves port everyone on board has to participate in an emergency drill. We were assigned to an outside area on an upper deck. From stem to stern there are three banks of elevators on the ship. This was the only time we experienced significant waits for the elevator.

The problem with being at the very front of the ship was the distance to the elevators. Each morning I ran my own obstacle course. The hallways were narrow to begin with but they were made even narrower because of the housekeeping carts I had to pass along the way. The carts had rubber wheels protruding out from their sides, presumably to minimize damage if a cart were to run into a hallway wall. Unintentionally, I used them occasionally while navigating down the hall. The thresholds in the hallway were a bit bumpy but proved to be only minor annoyances probably because I was never going very fast.

Once we made it up to one of the main decks, I was able to get around very easily. We were able to watch Luna and Eli play in the splash pad. The pool area had a Jumbotron sized screen that continually played Disney movies (what did you expect?). Finding areas to lie in the sun and watch the ocean go by was never difficult.

During our five-day voyage we docked three different times. The ship did the bulk it's sailing during the night and spent the days at different ports of call. The first stop was Nassau in the Bahamas. Matthew was the only one to the check out the sites there. He reported back that it was mostly gift shops and a Margaritaville restaurant. I love a good tourist trap but we opted to use that time to explore the ship.

Breakfast and lunch were served buffet style. I secured a table for all of us while Sarah grabbed my food. Dinners were more traditional and we rotated each night among three different restaurants. There were two different serving times to choose from. We ate at 5:30 but there was an 8:00 serving as well. Our waitstaff followed us from restaurant to restaurant each night so we always had the same team. After getting to know our habits at the first dinner, they always had our drink order waiting for us before we sat down for subsequent meals. Our waitresses' name was Denise and she was from Mexico. She was very personable and always wore a different colored frame for her glasses. The menu changed depending on the restaurant and it was always delicious.

Our second stop was the first of two Disney owned private islands. The Fantasy had a capacity of just over 4000 passengers and it seemed like most of them got off here. Like most things Disney, disembarking from the ship was a smooth, easy process. The gangplank was very wide and not very steep which made it easy for me to get on and off the ship. This island was very accessible for me and I could easily watch everyone frolic in the Caribbean.

My experience at the second Disney island was quite different. The boardwalks that I needed to get around were very short and quickly turned into beach sand. I could not see any of the beachgoers from my vantage point. There were "sand wheelchairs" available but I would have had to transfer into them and it would have been very difficult for someone to push me through the sand. We didn't see anyone using them. At each stop, passengers were instructed to be back on the ship by 5:30. As far as I know, no one got left behind.

Luna's love for princesses turned to uncertainty when she had a chance to get her photograph taken with them. She explained to Andy that she was surprised they were "real people". It didn't stop me though! I met Snow White, Cinderella, Jasmine and Belle.

Luna did enjoy the characters! She (and I) got our pictures taken with the big six; Mickey Mouse, Minnie Mouse, Donald Duck, Daisy Duck, Goofy and Pluto. We ran into those characters several times during our trip. Mickey wore a captain's uniform while on the boat but when relaxing on one of the islands he dressed more casually in a Hawaiian shirt. We also saw, Chip and Dale, some of Snow White's dwarf friends as well as Captain Hook along with his first mate, Smeeg. Hook was actually a pretty nice guy. I think he gets a bad rap! Each of our new friends have excellent penmanship and I'm sure Eli and Luna will treasure their autograph books for years to come. Most importantly the birthday girl, Sarah, had a great time and she is already planning another Disney adventure when the grandchildren are older

*The future belongs to those who believe
in the beauty of their dreams*

—Eleanor Roosevelt

CHAPTER 17
Where Are They Now?

You must be asking, "How are two people who had lived in Michigan for 58 years surviving life in Columbus, Ohio?" Honestly, it's not too bad. Having Andy, Alyson, Luna and Eli only seven miles away certainly takes some of the sting out of it. Yes, they are way over the top for their Buckeyes. We are amazed by how many people that grow up here tend to stay here. I can't tell you how many people Sarah and I have met that were born here, went to school here and now raise their family here. No one leaves here! (Insert your own inbreeding joke).

The Columbus area is vibrant and very clean. The breadth and quality of the medical care through the University is top-notch. Yes, they are way over the top for their love of the Buckeyes but since we lean more towards the Spartans than the Wolverines, we are treated with considerably less loathing. One of the first medical professionals I met when we arrived noticed my Spartan sweatshirt and said, "the enemy of my enemy is my friend." Alexa tells me that this is a quote attributed to Captain Kirk from Star Trek. So, we've got that going for us, which is nice!

We have been to two events at the Schottenstein center which is on the OSU campus and is home to the University's basketball teams and other athletic teams. We saw a Cirque du Soleil show which was performed on ice. We also saw P!nk. Sarah knew how much I liked her and while I was in the hospital, she surprised me with tickets to her show. I can neither confirm nor deny that we were the only 60+ year olds in attendance but I can tell you it was a great show! She does a lot of aerial acrobatics during her shows and flew above us on several occasions. During the show, she talked about her relationship with her daughter. This melted Sarah's heart so she is now a fan of P!nk as well. The wheelchair accessible seats at Schottenstein were adjacent to each other, unlike the debacle we experienced at Michigan State University's Breslin Center.

In 2023, we bought tickets for the first and second round of the NCAA basketball tournament that would be played at Nationwide Arena. When we purchased the tickets, we had no idea which teams would be sent to Columbus. Incredibly, Michigan State was assigned to play at that site. The overall number one seed for the tournament, Purdue University would be playing there as well. The ticket package was for six games in total. Four games on a Friday and then two more on Sunday. Sarah and I went on Friday and witnessed something that had never happened in the history of the NCAA tournament. Number one seeded Purdue, lost to the 16th seeded team, Fairleigh Dickinson. FDU is located in Madison, New Jersey with a total undergraduate enrollment of barely 3000 students. In contrast, Purdue has over 39,000 undergrads. It was truly a David versus Goliath moment. I won't take up your valuable time teaching you the ins and outs of the college basketball bracket but trust me, this was a big deal!

Michigan State was not expected to do very well that year but we were pleasantly surprised when they defeated the University of Southern California on Friday. Andy went to the games with me on Sunday to see is alma mater in action. MSU surprised the pundits (as well as us) by defeating Marquette University and advancing to the Sweet 16.

We have also discovered a wonderful venue to watch live performances, the Ohio Theater. The theater is located directly across from the state of Ohio capitol building. Handicapped parking and seating areas work very well for there. Some of the plays we saw there include Hamilton, Jesus Christ Superstar and To Kill a Mockingbird

***

You have been introduced to a plethora of the important people in my life since my accident. I reached out to many of them to find out what they were doing now. Here's what I found out.

The Griswolds are now all in their 60s and they continue their annual tournament as well as participating in a Thursday night golf league. Many of them are enjoying their grandchildren just as Sarah and I do. There was one cancer scare in our group but it was caught early and he is in full recovery now. I keep in touch with all of them and they continue to be a great source of support and love for me. Every conversation ends with a heartfelt "I love you".

My surgeon, Dr. Colen, moved his practice to Florida. Sadly, he has been diagnosed with multiple sclerosis and is no longer able to perform surgery. I wear the hat similar to the one I first saw him in as a tribute to him every time we go out.

Dr. Ho is still at MFB as the medical director but is less hands-on with patients now. He kept true to his word. Everyone went home but he stayed there.

Ashley, the chipper young woman who was the first therapist I worked with at MFB has since earned her doctorate in occupational therapy and teaches classes at grand Valley State University in Grand Rapids, Michigan

Tracy, one of my physical therapists at Mary Free Bed, left MFB in 2022 and now works for Michigan rehab solutions. She works with the same types of patients she did at MFB; brain injuries, spinal cord injuries, amputees and trauma.

Becca, the tech I enjoyed the most while at MFB, went back to school and is now a nurse. She is married with two children and is without doubt is entertaining her patients while providing excellent care.

Diane, who worked with me in the pool retired two years ago and has now become an expert in flyfishing in northern Michigan.

Mambo, the woman who prayed over me in Swahili, used to spend six months each year working in her home country, Democratic Republic of

Congo (DRC). Her father fell ill and she brought him to the United States so he could get better health care. She no longer returns to the DRC because of ongoing dangerous conflicts in the region.

Leslie, the MFB nurse who made the covers for my Foley bag, is now a traveling nurse. She enjoys going all over the country but is sure to spend time with her three grandchildren with a fourth on the way.

Kara, the PT student/softball pitcher at MFB as her doctorate in physical therapy and is working at a facility called "Hulst Jepsen" full-time while also raising three girls under the age of 3! I have no idea how she pulls that off.

Troy, the hardest working tech at MFB, is still there, spreading cheer as he hustles through the hallways. He is very active on FB and we talk to each other through that medium quite often. A lot of the information I have about former MFB workers is from him.

Sophia, from my first outpatient rehabilitation center, STAR, sold that business and now owns a business called "Senior Care Authority". This company helps facilitate patients going from home healthcare into assisted-living programs. I made a point to ask her about her shoe collection. She told me that she had just moved in with her boyfriend and that he was "freaked out" by the number of shoes she had.

Mandy, from Level 11 in Grand Blanc is now the clinic manager at a rebranded therapy facility called "Rehab Without Walls".

Randi, Mandy's partner in mischief at Level 11 still works with Mandy as an assistant manager.

The team, the team, the team.
No person is more important than
the team

—Bo Schembechler

CHAPTER 18
The Story Behind the Story

Remember way back when I was still in ICU? Sarah and I decided that we wanted to turn my tragedy into something positive. We are doing our best to live up to that pledge. I created a YouTube channel called "The Optimistic Quadriplegic" Seriously, what else could it be called? It has kind of become my "brand" now. There are dozens of videos there that are all about the early years of my recovery. The Mary Free Bed staff has made a professional video about my story that you can find there. MFB also made a video in which several patients lip-synced to the lyrics of "Carry On". I make two appearances in that video, see if you can find me. I am certainly not an influencer with hundreds of thousands of followers but I do have over 125 and some of my videos have been viewed over 500 times.

I have done several motivational talks to groups about my situation and the importance of keeping a positive attitude. I was receiving so much positive feedback about how inspirational my talks were Sarah and I decided to try to reach a wider audience. This led to what you are reading right now.

In 2020 I started to write a book, more specifically, my memoir. I had never written anything longer than a college term paper let alone a full-blown book but all of the positive out pouring of support, convinced me that my story was one worth telling. Sarah and I prayed on it and we agreed that by hearing about my journey it could help others make it through the tough times they are facing.

After doing some research, I found out there are basically two ways to publish a book. The first is to use an established publishing house. There are only five of them and it is extremely difficult for a first-time author to get a book published by one of them. My name does not carry the cachet of James Patterson, Nora Roberts or J. K. Rowling.

The easier path to creating an actual book is through self-publishing. The biggest seller of self-published books is Amazon. Amazon has a book publishing arm called KDP. I had an advantage over fictional novel writers in that I already knew the story. I just had to retell it in an entertaining, informative and motivational way. The first hurdle was to get my story out of my head and onto a computer. This was a little bit more difficult for me since I did not have the ability to type on a keyboard. Sarah loves me but she was not about to take dictation of a 50,000-word book. Even she has her limits!

I found a software called Dragon. It allows me to use voice to text technology similar to what you have on your phone. However, Dragon does much more than Suri or Alexa. If I make a mistake while dictating, I can give it a command to "cut that" and I am able to start again where I left off. Dragon also helps me with spelling and grammar. If I forget to put a comma in a necessary place it will underline the location in blue that needs attention. It also alerts the when I need to include a possessive apostrophe or conversely alerts when I don't need one. Sometimes technology can be frustrating and Dragon just can't understand some of my words. When that happens, I use the command "spell it". I simply spell the word I need letter by letter and as the letters line up a list of possible words drops down. I can complete my word or I can select one of the words from the drop-down menu as it appears. This feature is also handy when using names or titles that are spelled unusually. For example, you will recall that one of my aide's name was Rylee. When I say her name Dragon prefers to spell it the more common way, Riley. Also, for this situation I can create my own little list of vocabulary words that Dragon will always refer to first. In the worst-case scenario I am still able to use the keyboard to type.

Sarah helped me with many details included in this book that TGA had stolen from me. I also consulted my own YouTube videos for some items. In total it took me about four months to complete what I thought was the book. Not so fast! What I had was a manuscript not a book. I still needed to format the book and create a cover. I outsourced those jobs using a website called Fiverr. Then yada, yada, yada "The Optimistic Quadriplegic", first edition, was posted for sale on Amazon in paperback and Kindle versions on 7/11/21. I had to pull out the yadas there because this is a book about the Optimistic Quadriplegic not the overwhelmed writer. The copy you are reading is the second edition published in 2025. Feel free to reach out to me if you would like more details about the entire process.

I look forward each day to writing. It gives me a real sense of purpose and it keeps my mind sharp. Since I have written this memoir, I have also published five novels.

- ***The United States of Analytics***-If the United States government supplied each citizen with free education and free medical care, would they also want to control how the money is spent? What if tests revealed that the combined DNA of you and your spouse would likely result in an expensive medical treatment for that child. Could they prevent you from having that baby?
- ***Magic Mirror*** - Women in multiple cities around the United States are being murdered in eerily similar ways. Strangled in their

homes, dressed in workout clothes and always in the presence of the latest phenomenon in home exercise, the workout mirror, which included your own virtual trainer.

- *DNA Deception* - Millions of people around the globe happily submit their most valuable piece of information, their DNA, in hopes of finding their long-lost relative. In the wrong hands, DNA could be used for our imaginable chaos. What could your government or employer do with this information? What could your enemies do with this information?

- *The Buskers* - Three strangers meet in Las Vegas during the dawn of MTV. Follow their journey as they unite and become a "one-hit wonder". Where do they go from there? Will they be famous or infamous?

- *Dead Ball* – Pickleball, a game that was played by senior citizens in retirement communities has quickly become a national sensation. As the game grew in popularity, more people brought more divergent personalities to the game. As in every facet of life, some people take things too far and chaos follows. The worst type of chaos is murder.

Marketing my books is much more difficult than writing them. I have sold more books face-to-face than through the Amazon site. It is much more effective to talk about my books directly than it is hoping a person reads the description and clicks on the link to purchase. Sarah and I have attended dozens of craft/book shows.

Attending the shows is quite a process and has earned Sarah yet another job title, vice president of marketing. I purchase copies of my book from Amazon at a discount and we sell them at shows. Several things are taken to each of these and guess who has to haul them? Sarah should probably join the Teamsters union.

Most importantly, are the books themselves. There are usually three very heavy totes filled with my books. Most shows provide a table but if we have to bring our own folding 6-foot table. A covering is placed over the table that hangs down over the front. Sarah hangs large copies of the covers of my books on the front of the table along with our price list and a sign that indicates we accept credit card payments. Easels are placed on the table to display the books. We also have a bowl of candy to help draw people in. Keep in mind that Sarah is the one that has to do all of these tasks. We are usually very busy during the shows and she never complains, at least not to me. The best time of year for bookselling are the shows leading up to Christmas. We go to a show in Grand Blanc each November and a huge show at Wings Stadium in Kalamazoo. Sarah gets to reconnect with dozens of people, including former students.

At a recent show I received confirmation that getting out and meeting people was helping others as well as myself. A woman stopped in front of our table and stared silently at our display. She pointed to the Optimistic Quadriplegic book and asked, "Is that you"?

When I told her it was, she started sobbing and gave me a hug. She said that she had been taking care of her son who has had Parkinson's for several years and it is very stressful for her. That day her sister insisted that she get out of the house and take a break. She ended up at the craft show not knowing why. She told me that God must have sent her there to meet me. It was very powerful.

In the process of writing my books I often use Google to research various items. If something nefarious ever happened to Sarah and the police investigated my searches I could be in a lot of trouble. Some of the things I have searched for include:

- How do you inject heroin?
- Which cities have the most murders each year?
- What does DNA stand for and how can it be used?
- What is the best drug to use in a drink to kill someone?
- What does the Oval Office look like?
- What are some lesser-known cities in China?
- What types of investigation are done at crime scenes?

Sometimes I ask Alexa these questions while I am in my den, then soon after Sarah will shout, "what was that one all about?" I can almost hear her shaking her head and rolling her eyes.

You can learn new things at any time in your life if you're willing to be a beginner. If you actually learn to like being a beginner, the whole world opens up to you

—Barbara Shur

Final Notes and Acknowledgments

My optimism was forged during those first days after my accident. Things could have been so much worse. My road towards recovery was made considerably easier because I chose to look forward positively rather than looking backwards and bemoaning my situation. With the help of my family and friends I will continue to live an optimistic life of faith, hope and love.

The people named in this book are only a tiny fraction of the outstanding people who have been part of my journey. It would be an impossible feat to list them all. I don't think any of you did it for recognition anyway. Please know your cards, emails, phone calls, prayers and unending support have meant the world to Sarah and I. The journey would've been a lot more difficult without your love and support. Now, more than ever, we don't hear enough about the kindness in the world but there is a lot of it out there and we appreciate everything that everyone has done and continues to do for us.

I am extremely thankful to all the medical profession that provided me with such outstanding medical care every step of the way. I have seen more than my share of specialists. Physiatrists, neurologists, wound care, podiatrists, infectious disease specialists, orthopedists, surgeons. Just about every "ologist" with the exception of gynecologist.

There may be one professional golfer reading this and wondering "Hey, what about me?" That would be Phil Mickelson. Sarah reached out to him and/or his people and told them my story. He/they responded very quickly and sent me an autographed picture and glove. Thanks, Phil!

If you could please do me the favor of completing a review of this book on Amazon, Goodreads or wherever you may have purchased this book. The algorithms that are used for promoting my book depend heavily on this piece of the puzzle. Thank you in advance for your help!

Our next project is training to become peer mentors at Ohio State's hospitals. We hope to help others work through their troubles and trauma by using our experiences. Finally, if you know of an individual or group that would benefit from hearing about my story, I would definitely like to help motivate people and lift their spirits if possible. Please feel free to contact me. I can be contacted through my Facebook page or email me at kstonestrong@gmail.com. My website is keith-stone.com May God bless each of you!

www.ingramcontent.com/pod-product-compliance
Lightning Source LLC
Chambersburg PA
CBHW051518120626
46551CB00012B/985